Live Free Live Young Live Happy

A Transformative Quest for Joy and Contentment

Dr. Gurpreet Kaur

Copyright © Dr. Gurpreet Kaur 2023
All Rights Reserved.

ISBN 979-8-89067-754-9

This is a need of present global scenario on 'How to live life'. A must carry guide for adolescents, every adult from all walks of life, every parent and every teacher. Regards for Gurpreet ma'am.
Radhika -Entrepreneur,
Logical Mathematics Coach, UAE

The book, 'Live Free Live Young Live Happy' resonates with today's global confusion & chaos on life's sound principles and ethics, lack of which is leading to unhappiness, disturbance of mind and serenity among the humanity especially youth. A must read for everyone everywhere for leading happy and youthful life.
Ruzual, Student Masters' degree in
University of South Australia, Australia

"Live Free Live Young Live Happy" strikes a chord with health enthusiasts, guiding them along a holistic path to wellness. This book, written by Dr. Gurpreet Kaur, combines philosophy and practical advice for a fulfilling life in a way that aligns perfectly with the priorities of health-conscious people. From "Disease and Ease" to "Anger Management, " the chapters provide deep insights into the mind-body connection and emotional equilibrium. In today's fast-paced society, the book's advice on maintaining physical health while fostering mental and emotional vitality is invaluable. This book enables its readers to live a vibrant and joyous life by emphasizing well-being strategies that resonate with a health-conscious audience. "Live Free Live Young Live Happy" is a guidebook for individuals seeking to attain holistic wellness by harmonizing their physical, mental, and emotional dimensions.

Best Wishes, "You are a star, proud of you. It's a very helpful work for entire humanity worldwide. "
**Dr. Aman Ahuja- M. D. (Medicine), MIAE,
MITS -Director, Physician & Heart Specialist,
Raj Hospital and Heart Centre, Consultant and Cardiologist,
Pahwa Hospital; Ex. Consultant -Hero DMC Heart Institute,
SPS Apollo Hospital, Orison Hospital**

This book by Dr. Gurpreet Kaur is an insightful guide for everyone who is oblivious about the universal truth of oneness and struggling to navigate the complex terrains of life and relationships.

Deep analysis and practical advice with relatable anecdotes by the author provides a road map for nurturing healthy relationships within the demanding present environment understanding the dynamics of love, friendship and human connection while emphasizing on empathy, open communication and resiliency, making it an indispensable resource for those seeking harmonious and meaningful relationships.

It would definitely help you in demystifying and fortifying the intricate web of human relationships with yourself, your partner, your mind and The Mighty Power.
**Mr. Aunali A. Rupani -Investment Banker & India
Head - Discover Oneness Foundation USA.**

A civilized, knowledgeable, literate, open minded, reasonable and sophisticated guide for the couples, professionals and youth starting from late teens.
**Harpinder & Amarpreet - A Computer faculty Sr. Sec.
students & a perfect homemaker resp., India**

The book's insights are presented in a manner that speaks directly to my age group, making them easily applicable to my personal life journey. "Emotional traps" navigates us to be emotionally strong and not to be delusional but practical in life. I recommend it strongly to all youngsters to start their journey of life in right direction. A big thanks, Gurpreet ma'am.
Michelle - Age 20, Chitkara University, India

The Book, "Live Free Live Young Live Happy" covers all the aspects of human needs.

Everyone wants to live Free, Young and Happy and the author has truly justified in her book, offering practical solutions to fulfil above requirement in eight chapters.

It starts with uniqueness of human being, which also helps One to achieve purpose of life and attaining fulfilment, while coming across various emotional traps, as it tells that… It all starts with the thoughts in mind and book helps in mastering the art of Manifestation.

It also discusses about connection of body with mind and how one can create a self healing environment.

Fifth chapter of the book beautifully covers the mechanism of relationship between couples with reference to communication, spirituality and sexuality.

One chapter of book talks about anger management and most important the eighth and the last chapter of the book talks about having connection with the Supreme Power.

In nut shell this book is a must read for everyone who is committing to take his life to next level.
CA Harpreet Singh Kharbanda - Asstt. Governer, Rotary, Dist. 3070, 2017 - 18 and 2022-23

The book is dedicated to all my human soulmates in this wonderful journey of life because I love you.

Let's see what the GenZ and their mothers are thinking about the book

"AS A TEENAGER, I loved reading this book. It is full of positivity and it teaches us how to balance our lives. I AM DEFINITELY GONNA RECOMMEND THIS BOOK TO EVERYONE IN GEN Z. I hope you'll give it a try. It's one of the best books in a while."
Samaira, age 18, aspiring student, Psychology, Canada

"The author has helped us focus on the task at hand erasing all energy-depleting things. Lots of love and respect."
Jasleen, age 20, Student, Seneca College, Canada

"This book bridges the gap between parents and teens. The perfect read."
Vinny, age 43, loving mother & wife, India

"Deeply peep into yourself & all your relations with the help of this book and be your own Relationship Counselor."
Jasmeet Kaur, age 45, mother of two teenagers, affectionate wife and DIL, India

"Perfect way of touching sensitivity of 'sex and relationships' the way parents and teachers want it for their late teens and adult children. LOVE, LOVE N LOVE.
Meenu, age 50, mother of 3 young adults, a Yoga teacher, India

Contents

About the Author

A Motivational Speaker & Humanitarian, Training & Counseling Consultant and Founder Director - R Trainers and Motivators (A T&D Venture that received many laurels including C.B.S.E. Empanelment for India & Abroad). Seasoned and Skilled professional who has touched more than two lac lives across Corporations, the Education Sector, the Banking Sector, Networking Institutes and Hospitals. She is having over 2 decades of experience with adults & children to develop vibrant personalities, groom entrepreneurship skills, reinforcing positive thoughts and providing life-saving solutions. She is a social worker with a vision to uplift the community through her unconditional services as a Rotarian.

She has facilitated inclusive adjustment of Indian and international students coming from diverse socio-economic and cultural backgrounds. She is on the panel of many esteemed Public and Private Organisations. She is a strong motivator with sound analytical, problem-solving, communication and interpersonal skills for Heads of organizations, professionals, parents, front-line staff, homemakers and students of all ages. Her areas of expertise include Training & Development and Soul Searching. Coaching human lives on Life skills is her love, duty and Call of life.

Foreword-1

Live Free Live Young Live Happy
By Dr. B. S. Bhatia

Live Free Live Young Live Happy is a dazzling synthesis of philosophy and spirituality that captures the essence of personal development and empowerment. This book by Dr. Gurpreet Kaur resonates profoundly with college|university students, executives, professionals, homemakers providing invaluable insights for their voyage of self-discovery. Its' eight chapters, which range from embracing individuality to nurturing resilient relationships and managing emotions, address the plethora of difficulties a human life face. This literary gem not only acknowledges the unique challenges confronted by young adults but it also offers practical advice to the experienced elderly. The chapters seamlessly connect significant ideas with relatable examples, ensuring readability. This book offers practical methods for stress management, emotional well-being and meaningful self connection that are especially relevant to the truthful and emotional rigours of our life.

"The phrase 'Live Free Live Young Live Happy' serves as a guiding light for adults in every walk of life navigating the complexities of relationships and personal development. Taking support of Holy Gurbani has illuminated this book with spiritual wisdom. Author has skilfully crafted a transformative guidebook that invites readers to embark on a voyage of self-empowerment, self-acceptance, and inner peace".

Dr. B. S. Bhatia - Pro Vice Chancellor
RIMT University, Mandi Gobindgarh, Punjab, India

Foreword-2

Live Free Live Young Live Happy
By Dr. Dharam Singh

"Live Free Live Young Live Happy" is a transformative guide to achieving genuine happiness and meaningful relationships, penned by Dr. Gurpreet Kaur. The book is a compelling journey through various life dimensions, offering practical wisdom and insights for a fulfilled existence.

The book's sections delve into essential aspects of personal growth and well-being. "Unique You" advocates self-discovery and acceptance, guiding readers to embrace their authenticity and find purpose. "It's All in the Mind" explores the power of positive thinking, enabling readers to overcome limiting beliefs and unlock their potential. "Emotional Traps" provides tools to navigate complex emotions, helping readers find constructive outlets and break free from negativity.

"Dis-ease and Ease" emphasizes the mind-body connection, offering holistic approaches to physical and mental well-being. "Couple, Sex, and Marriage" tackles relationship dynamics, highlighting effective communication and intimacy for lasting partnerships. "Enraged Relationships" explore into conflict resolution, fostering understanding and harmony.

"Anger Management" equips readers with strategies to handle anger and develop emotional intelligence. Finally, "Befriending

God" explores spirituality and inner growth, encouraging readers to deepen their connection with their beliefs.

"Live Free Live Young Live Happy" by Dr. Gurpreet Kaur presents an inspiring roadmap to true happiness and fulfilling relationships. With practical advice and thought-provoking anecdotes, the author navigates readers through the complexities of life, helping them overcome challenges, nurture relationships and cultivate a joyful and purposeful existence.

"Live Free Live Young Live Happy" is an invaluable companion for those seeking personal growth and genuine happiness.

With abundant blessings,

DR. DHARAM SINGH

Member (Academic), Educational Tribunal, Punjab,India

President - Bhartiya Yog Sansthan, District Ludhiana (South)

Former Principal, SCD Government College, Ludhiana

Former Registrar, JGND Punjab State Open University, Patiala

Preface

Live Free Live Young Live Happy:
(A Transformative Quest for Joy and Contentment)

I believe, the search of pleasure and fulfilment is more important than ever in today's world with all its ongoing obstacles, uncertainties and crushing expectations. We all yearn, at our cores to live lives filled with meaning and fulfilment. Yet it may be challenging to make sense of our feelings, our relationships and our own thinking. If you're on a quest to learn more about yourself and make positive changes in your life, Live Free Live Young Live Happy can be a beacon of hope, providing deep insights and actionable advice to help you find inner peace, strengthen your connections with others and create a more fulfilling life.

As we set out on this life-altering adventure, the book first sheds light on the "Unique you" because 'to be yourself in the world that is constantly trying to condition you to someone else is the greatest accomplishment of the mankind'. Moving forward, you get alert on the nebulous emotional pitfalls into which we might so easily fall in the book's chapter "Emotional Traps". You are encouraged to delve deeply into your emotions, learning more about where they come from and how they shape our lives, from the grip of fear and self-doubt to the allure of attachment, wrath and hatred. You will learn to recognise and break free of these detrimental tendencies with the use of personal experiences, keen observation, psychological research and compassionate counsel. By strengthening our capacity for emotional intelligence and resilience, we may liberate ourselves from the constraints that prevent us from developing and enjoying our full potential.

With this newfound knowledge of feelings in hand, the book explores the intriguing world of the mind in "It's all in mind", mind being a potent tool that creates our reality and drives our behaviour. The power of optimistic thought is highlighted here. As we gain the ability to direct our ideas and beliefs towards the achievement of our goals, we get insight into the full scope of their influence on our life. You are urged to have an optimistic outlook and see difficulties as learning experiences. This revolutionary strategy will encourage you to take ownership of your life, destroying limiting beliefs and planting the seeds for change and growth.

The state of our bodies and minds are equally important in our pursuit of contentment. The book emphasises the need for a comprehensive perspective on 'restlessness' in the chapter "Dis-ease and Ease," which examines the close relationship between mind, body and body. Building a happy life requires a multifaceted approach that prioritises one's physical, mental, spiritual and emotional health. Readers are given realistic practical tips for achieving total health and vitality setting them on the path of pleasure, bliss, happiness & foremost -to be easy with themselves.

The complex network of relationships we build throughout the course of our lives is fundamental to our very being. The intricacies of romantic unions are discussed in the book's chapter titled "The Couple, Sex and Marriage," which acknowledges that these relationships may bring tremendous joy as well as hardships. Key aspects in maintaining happy and healthy relationships include open lines of communication, emotional support and closeness. You are encouraged to learn more about your significant others so that you may create a loving and respectful atmosphere that brings out the best in your relationships.

The chapter "Enraged Relationships" looks at the darker side of relationships, which may put a pall over even the most loving ones, here, you are given helpful advice and concrete strategies for resolving rage in a healthy way. Anger and resentment are two emotions that may do serious damage to the stability of your relationships; which is in detail touched in its' chapter "Anger Management". Restoring peace, rekindling love, and maturing as a person through life's inevitable ups and downs may all be achieved when individuals learn to handle difficult emotions with empathy and understanding.

The chapter "Befriending God" is a surprising and deep detour into the spiritual sphere for "Live Free Live Young Live Happy. " Spirituality is a path that may be pursued by anybody regardless of their religious or philosophical learnings, in hopes of finding peace and meaning through a relationship with a POWER larger than themselves. Spirituality encourages introspection, a process through which people might discover a profound calm in life's riddles.

My dear, you are encouraged to accept your individuality, cultivate emotional freedom and set out on a path towards a more fulfilling and fulfilled existence with the help of this caring and motivating guide. Seeking joy evolves into something more substantial: a way of life. Emotional acuity, optimistic outlook, whole-person health and supportive connections all work together to help people live meaningful fulfilling lives. Regardless of one's background, Live Free Live Young Live Happy can serve as a universal road map to your success and contentment.

This is a book for individuals who are curious about the world and want to learn more about who they are and where they fit within it. This book bridges the gap between timeless ideas and modern issues by drawing on the insights of ancient philosophies and cutting-edge scientific findings. Let us, as we make our way through the pages of this life-altering book, accept the challenge to live young, to keep the enthusiasm and wonder of our youth and to face the world with an open mind and a willing heart.

Let us break free from the chains of negativity and confinement, allowing our thoughts to fly above and beyond our previous expectations. Let us, above all else, strive to enjoy life to the fullest keeping in mind that satisfaction and fulfilment come from inside and that happiness is more than the absence of suffering.

To sum it up, Live Free Live Young Live Happy is a remarkable look into the boundless potential of the human heart and mind. Inspiring readers to take the first steps on a path towards a more genuine, joyful and satisfying existence. May this book be a constant companion on your individual transformational journey. Let joy be something you experience every day rather than something you wish for; the ability to enjoy life without restraint and with unabashed contentment is a gift we each possess. In an endeavor to present you, your own self (which is at core - smart, simple and stable) to Live Free, Live Young and Live Happy.

With Love,
Dr. Gurpreet Kaur
Humanitarian
Motivational Speaker
Training & Counseling Consultant
Director-R Trainers & Motivators

Live Free Live Young Live Happy:
(A Transformative Quest for Joy and Contentment)

<u>Dr. Gurpreet Kaur</u>

Chapter 1

The Unique You

"This is me and I respect myself, I Love who I Am - most respected, most loving,

GOD'S BELOVED CHILD."

Believe in Yourself

Be confident. Be you. You cannot copy others. You cannot breathe in others' clothes. You are unique in your own self. Others may give their thousand of opinions to instill fear, insecurity and doubt in you but always listen to your inner voice and firmly believe in your originality. Be positive, ultra optimist and open-minded. Always send good thoughts to all, bless all. As thoughts travel faster than you, so they reach a person anywhere in the world to nourish your relations. Try to make a positive difference in everybody's life. Rise in love in all relations. Do not be possessive but loving and warm. You should be a solution minded person with a good eye not a problem finder with a bad eye. Think from other's perspective while they are conveying something to you. My friend, few people bring happiness when they enter our life and few when they leave. The choice is ours who would we like to be. Increase your limit to love humanity daily. Build your capacity to accept all... but believe my friend, you cannot make your loved ones' happy with your compromises. Everyone feel imprisoned and suffocated with IMPOSED decisions. And your suffocation will make you sad and depressed. At the end.... you will be agitated and not able to deliver happiness to those for whom you have given up your dreams. We cannot make the whole world happy however good we are. Accept it now. I am saying it with experience. So, take the responsibility of making yourself happy first.

> ***Ideas are no one's monotony. Whatever you wish, whatever you dream, whatever you hope to achieve, will be YOURS, only; IF YOU BELIEVE IN YOURSELF.***

When your intentions are true then remember, TAKE responsibility of your actions. Take stand when you are right. You are responsible for your actions not for the actions of others. If somebody is imposing his/her ideas on you, which doesn't match your philosophy of life, please be firm otherwise you are going to compromise on your peace and happiness forever. So don't panic & don't be fearful. Don't think what others will think or what others will do, when WHAT you think according to you is right. (Listen to all, don't react but follow your own inner voice confidently).

> ***"Right means which heals, which constructs, which makes you happy, resolve your conflicts, change your perception, makes you respectable, loving, compassionate, solves your life's purpose and DOES NOT HARM anyone."***

While doing Self-Introspection, see that are you moving towards elevating **Good Qualities in you** -Truth, Patience, Loyality, Humbleness, Confidence, Compassion, Empathy and Open communication. And are you moving away from **Toxic characteristics in you** - Attachment, Cheating, Illusion, Harshness, Restlessness, Discrimation and Operating from Ego.

- Be clear, Be expressive, Be bold, Be right and Be power. Remember : Universe will help you.
- Remember, Oneness prevails everywhere and in everyone.
- Bring the change with YOUR boldness.
- Be the change YOU want to see in others.

> ***BELIEVE** - You are Power, You are Positive Change, You are Love, You are energy. You are Free Soul. You are a Genius. You are very beautiful.*

While on this journey, have Zero Expectations from others & full faith on two powerful energies, you-yourself and dear God. He always think best for you, **that is why** many a times we don't get what we desire but we definitely are given what we deserve. We are short sighted, we can't see what is God's call or What God is planning for us. SO, DON'T EVER GIVE UP. Appreciate everything and expect nothing. Expectations hurt. Please don't expect. Really!Yes. Wanna do something for someone...please volunteer but unconditionally.

While struggling on conflicting opinions with your near ones, opt for open - honest expression of your feelings & emotions with the concerned person in the most humble way to develop understanding on mutual grounds. Please don't suffer inside you and feel helpless. Along with that share your point of view with God. He will help you in accomplishing your goal. He will remove all the barriers coming on your way. And when you move with your inner voice, YOU WILL EXPERIENCE LIFE IN YOU. While experiencing life, if not a fruitful experience, surely a meaningful lesson will be learnt. Confide in Superpower before confiding in any mortal being. You will be given solutions in the form of some person approaching you for help or a message you shall receive on any media. Believe me, my friend, its'true. I'm sure, there will be positive change in your situation but again, if not, then keep on praying for the best results and acceptance at the core level..

Holy Sri Guru Granth Sahib Ji, Ang 281

ਮਾਨੁਖ ਕੀ ਟੇਕ ਬ੍ਰਿਥੀ ਸਭ ਜਾਨੁ ॥

मानुख की टेक ब्रथी सभ जानु ॥

Mānukẖ kī tek barithī sabẖ jān.

ਦੇਵਨ ਕਉ ਏਕੈ ਭਗਵਾਨੁ ॥

देवन कउ एकै भगवानु ॥

Ḏevan ka⁼o ekai bẖagvān.

Reliance on mortals is in vain - know this well.

The Great Giver is the One Lord God.

By His gifts, we are satisfied,

and we suffer from thirst no longer.

The One Lord Himself destroys and also preserves.

Nothing at all is in the hands of mortal beings.

Understanding His Order, there is peace.

Because if you stay timid in taking action, it will lead to confirming your belief that your existence in this life is faulty when, believe me, this world needs your original self only to contribute to their well being & to make visible elevating difference in their lives. Please don't wait anymore. Open up. Let the universe know that you are available.

> Think **Big**
> Think **Fast**
> Think **Ahead**

When we remove our negativity, automatically we discover **GOD INSIDE US**.

> *Always remember- successful people can't relax on chair. They relax by work. They sleep with a dream, awake with commitment and work towards goals.*

That's the spirit of life, my dear and trust me, you have that spirit.
- ✓ Follow & focus on purpose and goal of your life. You will give in abundance and you will get in abundance.
- ✓ Reduce/minimize dependencies.
- ✓ Do right thing at the right time.
- ✓ Practice perseverance.
- ✓ If above is not followed, energy is drained and we are not able to reach our goals. Energy if drained → Goal go away.

> **Stress, Guilt, Judgement about others, Self-doubt, Blame, Fear, Remembering Past, Confusions, Misunderstandings, Unresolved issues – drain our PRECIOUS ENERGY**

It doesn't mean that we are going to think evil about anyone. Nobody is bad, wickedness resides within us. PRAY GOD TO BANISH IT.... PRAY. He will be your mentor.

Holy Sri Guru Granth Sahib Ji, Ang 728

ਹਮ ਨਹੀ ਚੰਗੇ ਬੁਰਾ ਨਹੀ ਕੋਇ ॥

हम नही चंगे बुरा नही कोइ ॥

Ham nahī change burā nahī koᵁe.

I am not good; no one is bad.

Remember, my friend, He (Dear God) alone saves us!

2. Respect the uniqueness in you-

Nobody is superior, Nobody is inferior, but nobody is equal either, people are simply unique, incomparable, you are you, I am I. People will let you down in this life, promises will be broken, you should expect less of others trust more on yourself. Don't let yourself suffer because of inferiority complex, superiority complex and insecurities of other fellow beings. Yes, you can help them in overcoming these negative emotions with your unconditional love and warmth but please you are not allowed to be a prey to this negativity in others. My nice friend, You are achiever who is going to be and do great things in life. Keep filling your heart with great and inspiring thoughts and you will see powerful results. Life is meant to be lived for deep meaning and true purpose.

<u>Confidence building concepts;</u>

- Stop comparing yourself to others.
- Keep your thoughts positive.
- Accept all compliments with thank you.
- Fill yourself with positive input.
- Associate with positive people.
- List your past success.
- Celebrate your qualities.
- Do good deeds for others.
- Find your passion.
- Be yourself and be proud of it.

Every personality has whole universe in it with all of its' positivity and all of its' negativity. Our human journey starts from a newly born positive baby to the conditioned negative grown up, as we proceed in this journey. When we realize our negativity, then it's important to get rid of it fast to get positive again to enjoy our own vibrant personality. Also, when we feel ourself getting trapped into the negative world of people on whom we are dependent for our emotional strength, Be alarmed. Do try to help them get rid of their toxicity but you are not God to change their destiny. So pray for them but focus on your positivity and confidence. Please don't let these two powers shatter, friend.

There is nothing which can't be achieved. There is no fear that can't be conquered. Develop pursuasive skills. Let your voice be Heard. Be Confident. Be YOU.

3. <u>Be your own best friend.....</u>

"We have to learn to be our best friend because we fall too easily into the trap of being our own worst enemies"

You have the power........

You have the power to become confident, if you want to, and if you go about it the right way. Everyone has this power and it doesn't matter how lacking in confidence you are now. You can change your way of thinking. You can use your imagination differently, you can alter your way of speaking. You can let go off destructive habits and change your behaviour, you can do all this now, from this moment on. Then over time... your confidence will grow and you'll feel better and better about yourself with each passing day.

> ➤ Always live in high spirits. Don't let the fear of being unaccepted stop you. Chase your dream. Value your contribution at all levels. Be original and express your ideas. Keep on contributing at all levels- Self front, Home front, Societal front & be proud of that.

4. <u>Don't see yourself through others' lens-</u>

> ➤ Happiness is the choice. It is there deep within you. Whether you would like to be imprisoned by someone's judgements/ opinions/expectation of you or would like to live free and live young.
>
> ➤ So, Be you, love yourself / love your uniqueness. Chase your fear. 90% of it don't even exist.
>
> ➤ Chase fear, address it and attack it.
>
> ➤ Chase dream, imagine & believe then fulfil.

➢ Walk through the judgements of others with grace. Be the most positive and pure person who speaks truth, is non judgemental, who wants to live and let other live.

➢ Nobody is going to feel the pain you are going through. So, you only have to express and give voice to your dreams and choices. If you don't conquer fear and chase your dream you will be a duck who keep on doing quack quack throughout life and you'll keep on living in pain. Don't try to prove yourself always. Of course, Give your reasons once but Remember, you cannot make everybody happy in this world. You cannot always meet everybody's expectation of you, their ideology of you. So, love your own uniqueness and wisdom and pray for everyone's happiness.

> *A person without a dream is broken winged bird who cannot fly.*

➢ Remember, my friend, God only help those who help themselves.

➢ Listen to your heart & soul. Listen to its voice. Whole world is waiting to support you.

➢ Have faith in God. Do your duties, Don't blame yourself on the basis of judgements of others.

> ➤ UNDESTAND: There are two categories of people ducks and eagles.
>
> Ducks are those who keep on complaining, finding faults with others, always blaming others for their miseries/helplessness and are pain for themselves and others around them. They are always imprisoned in worries and problems.

> ➤ Other category is eagle – they fly high over all the quack-quack of ducks, fly, see and amend the world. These are the people who do perform their duties very well, are responsible, give free space to all relations, are concerned but don't complain, blame and find faults with others. On the contrary, they are appreciative of others where they find good in others. They're solution minded. They are bold. They express themselves, they contribute and have utmost faith in God Almighty. The problem here is ducks, being close minded, are not able to digest the carefree nature of the eagles. Please, don't give power to the small minds of the ducks rather focus on your dreams.

➤ Bridge the gap between you & your dreams & start now. Who will bother about your hopes and dreams if not you.

➤ You cannot please everybody. You don't even have to justify yourself to everybody. Everyone has their own level of survival.

➤ Many survive at ducks level but eagles feel suffocated amongst ducks. Each individual see clear through his/her customised lens. Acknowledge them and do what you feel best.

➤ Let your creative energy flow and stop expecting that ducks will understand you because they are so engrossed into their own self obsession that they just cannot see good in others. Understand, they have their own reasons to support their behaviour – their brought up and experiences. Keep on expressing yourself while empathising others and move on. Just don't forget to be polite, humble and kind. THEN FLY.

➤ Initially the ducks around you may highly complain but later when tired of quack- quack on you, they will find some other topic to complain and crib but those who truly love you and are concerned about you when they see you happy will also be happy and those who don't love you it really doesn't matter.

➤ Stop downrating yourself. There is no fear that can't be conquered either it's your career, dream or love.

5. "Be who you are and be willing to let others who they are."

We are all unique, but we cannot copy paste each other. Our uniqueness is important to solve our purpose on this earth. Like different flowers make a beautiful garden -Lotus, Marigold, Lily;

different vegetables add variety to our food and make it so tasty- Carrot, Beans, Lady finger, Capsicum, Potatoes etc. Similarly, we are all having our special set of properties/ characteristics / features/ traits with which we survive on this beautiful planet to serve some purpose bestowed to us by God Almighty. Always remember we are all unique in our own ways and we should cherish each other that way only. If we try to change others, it is just like beating your head against the wall and in this process we will be tired & frustrated & other persons will also feel agitated at our behaviour of changing them. So, total failure.

Again, **do anything** – a lot of yelling to change others, answer me, can we change Banana into Orange. **No, so fruitless effort.** Yes, it can be our choice whether we would like to eat Banana or not with all its properties? Is it good for us? Is it healthy for us? BUT we cannot convert it to same other fruit.

So, either you complain, fight, yell at other people for them to change and in turn become yourself as rebellious, aggressive and irritated.

OR

You accept the other person as he/she is and GRADUALLY develop strong bonds with him/her, if required as per your life situation & cherish each other's strengths & unique properties.

*I am not in this world to live up to your expectations. You are not in this world to live up to mine. I am I and you are you. Be the most kind, humble and empathic human but **BE YOU**

You are power, you are +ve change,

You are love, you are energy.

You are free soul.
Do not compel others to be like you, accept them the way they are.
And accept yourself the way you are.
The prayer I should do daily. Dear God, amend me, elevate me, strengthen me to contribute in everyone's life. Help me develop amicable relations with everyone with my soft skills and wisdom given by you.

6. <u>Focus on your SELF IMAGE-</u>

Self image set the boundary of your personal accomplishment.

We have two images of our self. One is the external image, which shows up in the way we walk, talk, dress etc. and the other is the internal image, how we see ourselves in our mind. The internal image dictates our personal results, for example, a poor self image will show up as poor results in life whereas a positive, strong self image will deliver positive, strong results. Our self image is built partially by our genetics but most importantly by the way we grow through our childhood. If a child is raised with praise that child tends to grow into someone who likes herself, who understands herself and who has a positive self image. A child raised in an atmosphere of negativity and criticism tends to be super critical of self, feels inferior and doesn't really understand self: has a poor self image.

> ***However, we have the ability to improve our own image.***

There is an image of perfection within each person, right at the center of his or her consciousness. The creative faculties we each have are often buried under piles of doubt, insecurities and we have to master and remove those negativities to allow the perfection to shine though. A person can achieve that by studying the self because the more we understand, our own self, the better the image we have of our self.

Moreover, TO CHANGE the results we are achieving in life, we have to examine our self images. Is it consistent with the outcomes we want? If not, create a new self image. Consciously and deliberately choose the kind of person you want to be. Create a written description in the present tense; this is also known as "imagined reality". Make yourself the star of your own movie script. Immerse yourself in the role and over time become the character you wish to portray.

> **THE RIGHT SELF IMAGE IS CRITICAL TO YOUR SUCCESS.**

7. Its' always your choice to be a Victim or Victor-

Our greatness is found not by chasing our dreams of a perfect life nor from running away from what scares us the most, but by anchoring ourselves deeply in this moment and every moment as it unfolds. Every test in our life makes us bitter or better, every problem comes to break us or make us. The choice is ours whether we become VICTIM or VICTOR. Never cry for the person who hurts you.... just smile & say, 'Thanks for giving me a chance to learn from the experience'. Don't stuck to one relationship or one event. Move ahead. Universe is very big. It needs your uniqueness. You will definitely find the appropriate company in accordance to your thoughts and current level of awareness. This new association will keep you happy, motivated and blissful.

8. Enjoy your own company-

You are love, compassion, courage, enthusiasm, honesty and blissful health.

<u>Discover yourself / Reinvent yourself</u>

Ask Yourself …..

1. Who am I ?

2. Am I living Right?

3. Where is my destiny….. what am I chasing and looking for… ?

4. What do I need to be happy and stressfree and How… ?

5. Why I have been chosen for the sufferings?

> *Change the perception and change the game of your life. You should be clear about difference between fear from God and fearlessness…. where to draw the boundary.*

> *Be you…. No one can replace you. You are the best. You are a solitaire.*

Keep asking yourself - What harm do I make to myself when I resist my abundance nature?

So, Evaluate yourself & keep checking the change.

Everyday relax and imagine the effect of updated, positive beliefs on your life. 'See' and 'Feel' yourself behaving differently as your confidence improve. Whenever you get an opportunity to put your new beliefs into practice, act as if they are definitely true.

> *I firmly believe you came into the world to accomplish something big and not something small or insignificant. That's not worthy of you. You came here to make a major contribution to life on this planet.*

9. Take a fresh look at the goals you listed in your notebook.

Are they still relevant? Or what else would you like to achieve?

Modify your list if appropriate. Write them down. PRINT THEM IN CAPITALS. Use clear language avoiding nebulous words and phrases such as 'I want to help people' Exactly how do you want to help them?

Aim high, but bear in mind that many people with low self esteem make unrealistic demands on themselves, they become frustrated by the gap between their aspirations and their actual accomplishments. Be realistic for example, YOU may be concerned about homeless people, but you can't house them all personally nor raise enough money to solve the problem on your own.

Concentrate on what you can do, and don't assume that if you can't save the whole of human kind, you've failed. Take each goal in true and list all the benefits that achieving it will bring to you, your family and the wider community. Remember, the more benefits you can identify, the greater the pulling power of your goal.

A real case study

A girl in the pursuit of making her family proud of her, kept on studying the subjects she didn't cherish and aspired for unrealistic goals as per her family's dreams. She, one day ended up in frustration, migraine and ulcers.

One fine day, her mother helped her in gathering all the strength in pursuing the goals in life as per her own cherished dreams, without bothering about anybody else's happiness but hers. She switched to her favourite subjects in Masters and achieved Doctorate degree with full ride scholarship in Organisational behaviour. Of course, she made her family proud but not at the cost of her own happiness and comfort.

> *"Cherish the freedom to be yourself. Be guided by your inner voice and do what you believe.". Sing, Dance and embrace life to the full."*

10. Be an Effective Communicator-

Work on youself for achieving Assertive Communication

Passive Communication

When using passive communication, an individual does not express his/her needs or feelings. Passive individual often do not respond to hurtful situations and instead allow themselves to be taken advantage of or to be treated unfairly,

Traits of Passive Communication;

1. Poor Eye Contact.

2. Allow others to infringe upon their rights.

3. Softly Spoken.

4. Allow others to take advantage.

Aggressive Communication

Aggressive Communication violate the rights of others when expressing their own feelings and needs. They may be verbally abusive to further their own interests.

Traits of aggressive communication;

1. Use of criticism, humiliation and domination.

2. Frequent interruptions and failure to listen to others.

3. Easily Frustrated.

4. Speaking in a loud or overbearing manner.

Assertive Communication

Assertiveness is defined as, "someone who is confident and is not frightened to say what they want or believe. "

Communicating your ideas and feelings in a calm, direct and respectful way whilst respecting equally the other person's views.

Assertiveness begins with the premise that your wants or needs are as important as someone else's.

Why Be Assertive?

✓ Increase the chances of your needs being met.

- ✓ Deliver better outcomes, especially in difficult contexts.
- ✓ Help create the conditions where you can influence others positively.
- ✓ Make you more effective in achieving outcomes.
- ✓ Reduce frustration- you are not left with the feeling that you didn't say | express what you wanted to.
- ✓ Develops your own self-confidence.

The Crux;

Be Positive- About yourself without lessening another persons' opinion.

Be clear -About what you want, your opinions and feelings.

Stand up- Be willing to stand up for your rights in an assertive way.

Respect -The rights and views of other people.

Keep - Calm, comfortable and confident.

Appropriate- Body language, being relaxed, maintaining eye contact, steady voice.

Seek- A resolution which is Win—Win.

A real case study

A married woman was expected to speak passively to the demands of her in laws family culture without giving her own opinions.

Husband and mother-in-law tried to impose family rules with aggression upon her.

One fine day, she felt imprisoned in her own self and gradually developed confidence to be assertive. She expressed herself with confidence, took stand where needed and firmly started believing on her own soul calls.

Ultimately, she found universe to respond her in accordance to her originality and she got rid of all unhappiness and boredom of her life. Remember, during this journey, nowhere she violated any moral ethics.

> *Understand, my friend, communicate to express, to understand and to be understood. Be happy, young and free forever.*

11. The Unique You And Your Purpose In Life

Life is meant to be lived for deep meaning and true purpose.
My friend, talking about me, as on today, my purpose of life is to promote this book to make visible difference in every life. 5 years back from today, my passion was to make difference in every human life through my life changing sessions and I believe 10 years down the line, my definition of happiness would be a peaceful, solitary life in the country with the potential to be helpful to those who are not used to having it done to them.

Yours can be totally different and it is absolutely right as long as it is doing good to the humanity.

> *To pursue your own unique purpose of life, you need to carry out these 5 actions to simplify and smoothen the road to reach your destiny:*

1. ***Do Your Undones first.***

   Your vitality is being drained by things in your life that are producing "psychic drama," such as an incomplete will, a fitness regimen that hasn't been followed, a project that has to be completed but has been put off, a relationship that needs to be fixed and a spiritual endeavor that has gone unattended. You'll experience a surge of creativity, productivity, enthusiasm and calm once you correct and finish these.

2. ***Utilize the news.***

   The news in our day and age may be extremely divisive and harmful. All I'm suggesting is to never use the news as an escape but rather to further your progress. Consuming this knowledge in moderation will calm down your days by lowering inner noise and decreasing external turmoil.

3. ***Cleanse physical areas.***

   Stress arises from mess. Clearing up your surroundings will remove distractions and negativity from the areas where you spend the majority of your time. Go minimalist at home and donate all the possessions that clutter up your space. Moreover, knowing that you're helping those in need will make you feel good.

4. ***Bid Energy Thieves Farewell.***

   You can either live your highest life or surround yourself with drama-loving people but not both. Remove the critics, whiners, justifiers and doubters from your life right now! It is important for retaining your mental health. You should be clear whom to justify, whom to give one line answers and with whom to keep silent but smile. Your thinking, performance, enjoyment, and impact will all be revolutionized. Love them from a distance if they are family members. Alternately, interact with them once or twice a day or weekly, monthly or quarterly basis rather than frequently, depending on your relation with them. ***Right, because, what's good for your soul is good for the world.***

5. ***Get Wilder.***

By this, I mean spend more time outside and get away from the world. I can't even begin to describe how gorgeously this shifts our perspective, refreshes our intellect, and charms our spirit. The more we get to know nature, the more deeply alive and drama-free we feel. Being close to nature is definitely being close to dear God.

Chapter 2

IT'S ALL IN MIND - Know it, Tame it, Win it, Grow with it

ਮਨ ਤੂੰ ਜੋਤਿ ਸਰੂਪੁ ਹੈ ਆਪਣਾ ਮੂਲੁ ਪਛਾਣੁ ॥

Man Thoon Joth Saroop Hai Aapanaa Mool Pashhaan ||

O my mind, you are the embodiment of the Divine Light - recognize your own origin.

ਆਸਾ (ਮਃ ੩) ਛੰਤ (੧) ਪ:੧ - ਗੁਰੂ ਗ੍ਰੰਥ ਸਾਹਿਬ : ਅੰਗ ੪੪੧ ਪੰ. ੩

Raag Asa Guru Amar Das

1. <u>Befriend your own mind</u>

Our energy starts depleting and immunity becomes weak, viruses get a breeding place to work on if we go against our minds. If we make mind our best friend, then we can always have a disease free happy life and our family and fellow beings will also be happy with us.

Whom do we call friend- whose mind matches with ours. So, when our actions matches with nature of our mind, it means we are befriended. Let's understand **Nature of mind-** Mind always want to be Fresh, Speedy, Adventurous, Loving, Warm, Happy, Affectionate, Open, Creative, Energetic and Flexible. Mind is really Powerful and need to enjoy present, remain Active, Positive, Friendly, Enthusiastic and accept new challenges. Mind intrinsically long a loving authority to make it disciplined on daily life needs and abide by truthful holy knowledge. When anyone acts opposite to the nature of mind as mentioned –if he/she is indisciplined, lazy etc., is fearful about others, is envy of others' qualities, is unfriendly, have obsolete perception, think small, judge others', then mind is uneasy and it starts diseasing you. ***This brings rigidness in the body which turns into many diseases.***

> ***Act in accordance to the nature of Mind. 'Make Mind your Bestfriend'.***

Always remember: mind is very powerful. If I befriend with my mind, I can achieve anything in life. Mind should be my best friend but I should KNOW that mind being creative, active, intelligent, pure and positive is **also nasty at times**. So it's my duty as a **parent of mind to direct it in the right direction**. So, it is crucial to sit in person with your own mind and train it with your soft skills. It also require its' taming with God's teachings with disciplined meditation and service to humanity.

<u>Holy Sri Guru Granth Sahib Ji, Ang 266</u>

ਸਰਬ ਧਰਮ ਮਹਿ ਸ੍ਰੇਸਟ ਧਰਮੁ ॥

सरब धरम महि स्रेसट धरमु ॥

Sarab dharam meh saresat dharam.

ਹਰਿ ਕੋ ਨਾਮੁ ਜਪਿ ਨਿਰਮਲ ਕਰਮੁ ॥

हरि को नामु जपि निरमल करमु ॥

Har ko nām jap nirmal karam.

Of all religions, the best religion is to chant the Name of the Lord and maintain pure conduct.

Of all religious rituals, the most sublime ritual

is to erase the filth of the dirty mind in the Company of the Holy.

Mind's nature is to keep on wavering. And because of our mood swings, we are not able to live free, young, stable and in bliss. If we tell our condition to anyone in the world, they judge, inspite of that, of course, this is the psychological first aid, however, not a permanent solution to attain a state of bliss. Because people have their own limitations- own perception, biasness, personal experiences, bend towards some relation, insecurity, fear and affection, so the solution may not be so perfect but God is limitless, so pray to Him for any weakness that you want to overcome. He will definitely come to rescue you.

Only God's protection can save us from the waves of mind like umbrella protects us from rain. When we go into protection of God, He takes the responsibility of your mind and one fine day our mind get stability.

We all get multiple thoughts in a day and during night according to the information stored in our subconscious mind. It is important to slow down the speed of our thoughts. Also, It is important to train the mind to dwell in present activities in hand, rather than focusing on the past events/ thoughts/ problems. Meditation helps us in bringing rest to mind so that it can focus in the present. It also gradually clear the information stored in subconscious mind which is of no use to us in the present scenario.

Meditation brings us peace of mind, serenity and tranquility. We are able to change the quality of our thoughts and choose right association by meditating on God. Now, the Choice is ours.

2. <u>Win your mind</u>

Our thoughts are produced according to the information we see, hear and speak during the entire day.

Whatever we think regularly is converted to reality one day. It is the truest of the true, my friend. Our repeated thoughts with its' images manifest the reality. Think Right.

<u>Real life cases</u>

1. A boy dreamt regularly of doing something big in life and he became a successful Chartered Accountant passing through the challenges of job, family and financial crunch.

2. A Teenager who manifested physical intimacy with a close relative in her thoughts for long, was one day physically close to him.

3. A woman manifested hatred for her mother-in-law for long and a day came she started abusing her on just a tinkle of her thought about her.

4. A boy who manifested thoughts of getting placed in leading International Corporate, cracked the same at the age of 22.

5. A middle aged woman when engrossed in thoughts about sex most of the times, manifested serenity with the help of regular meditation and she gradually overcame her discomfort.

Winning your mind. How?. Start by acknowledging your thoughts, address your thoughts with concern, weigh pros and cons on the scale of universal moral values, convince your mind for the right option. Mind will agree. When mind is involved in decision making, it willingly accepts. Mind has a parent child relationship with you. When child is involved in any kind of decision making, it does not rebel, there is UNDERSTANDING. We need to develop understanding with our own mind.

Let's take a situation here:

You have developed hatred for some person due to abc reasons. You envision all interactions with that person in past as situations to justify hatred for that person, in short, the memories with her, justify your mind behaviour to hate her the moment you see her or think about her.

The moment mind is convinced that it is justified in hating that person it will wait for minor stimulus to enter into conflict with that person, to yell, to complain, to vomit all the poisoning words which mind has thought repeatedly. Then the person least bother that these actions are being carried in front of abc relations. Mind forgets who is present there. What to do?

1st thought need to be stopped. Working has to be done on the 1st thought. We need to channelize that 1st thought.

How?

1. Mind is attached towards –ve 1st thought.
2. Write it on paper. Acknowledge that Thought.
3. Agree with the mind that it is right..... it's feelings are right........ agree with mind.
4. Now, consequences of that thought... if pursued, have to be discussed with mind.

Let mind sit in front of you and start dicussion... Ask your darling Mind, What if this thought start making thought patterns ? What will be the consequences? Where will these thought patterns lead you.... lets see....

1. I don't like this person....
2. I just cannot see this person
3. How much I hate this person …
4. I feel like killing this person…

    So, ask yourself…WHERE IS IT LEADING YOU ????

5. Make it understand the consequences.... Convince the mind about devasting consequences of this single –ve thought...... say to your lovely mind...... you're right my friend....... but what is the use of carrying this thought... when it will not give good /amicable results and will lead to a very difficult life.
6. Now- Tell the mind strongly.....

Can I afford to take these kind of consequences again & again. Will I be able to save my reputation with these kind of results.

What is the cost I have to bear for the consequences ? Can I afford the results of these negative thoughts at the cost of my family, children, self image.... tell it strongly to your mind.

Then, mind will understand & next time will act as your best friend.

The moment you are about to pick up a negative thought... mind will remind you not to do the same.... for your our good....

Henceforth, It will act as a watchful power towards choosing your thoughts when prior, it was your biggest enemy in choosing only –ve thoughts for you.

> ***Once mind is convinced, It will work in your favour. The result will be, your mind will automatically develop coping mechanism in the ways of let go, to ignore, to be patient, to be tolerant and not to over think.***

3. <u>Educate your mind to lead life with zero problems</u>

Whatever world says, Be Non-reactive on other's thoughts and judgements. You are not them. You are you & you are on a very big purpose. You don't have time for reaction & Remember- You don't have control over other persons' thoughts also. But the good part is, you have complete control over your own personal life. So, listen whole heartedly to everyone but act according to your inner voice. Don't enter into arguments with anyone. Make them feel that they are really wise. You DO what your soul wants you to do.

Make positive changes in your own behaviour with honest efforts. That will be the right approach.

"If you don't react to the situation, no biochemical changes will occur inside you, no toxins will be produced in the body. So, remain calm in all situations, don't analyse. Just learn from the situation or a person and move ahead towards constructive actions."

Develop zero problems MINDSET

Peace of mind is achieved when there are no blames, no grudges, no judgements, no fear, no enmity, no analysis about other person's actions, thoughts or words. We need to put a very strong anti-virus on our mind and trust my friends, only the shield of God's name is strong enough to give us such a shield.

4. The state of your life is nothing more than a reflection of your own state of mind.

I met a man of 61 years old in one of my Motivational Sessions. I could see he wanted to open up with me so we sat in a corner of the Hall to talk. He started complaining about multiple negative emotions- fear, anxiety, depression, aggression, irritable behaviour since 15 years. He had bypass heart surgery few years back and was diabetic. He confessed that he did not take care of his crying mind from a long time and moreover it was not in his priority list. Now, let's try to understand. The state of mind is like a child who has fallen from his cradle and has hurted itself. It is bleeding now and mother is feeling guilty about it. The man has regrets now that he did not give good environment to his children and wife because of his negativity. He came hoping for help to make him bold, peaceful, happy, calm, cheerful and blissful. This was his ultimate goal now as he had already wasted his precious 15 years of his life.

I asked him this question, did he do anything to eradicate these negative emotions; opened up with a friend | visited a counsellor| changed his thoughts |lifestyle or behaviour. He said he did but it was half hearted efforts which did not bear any fruits. All efforts were wasted.

Just think, ***"when we suffer from a physical ailment we get it treated immediately but most of times... the situation is when our mind needs immediate attention but agony is we tend to delay it"***. And the most unfortunate part is that we are not aware that this crying mind is only going to lead to the physical ailments Kants along with negative state of our mind- irritability, pessimistic behaviour, aggression, frustration, isolation, loneliness.

ਭੋਲਾ ਵੈਦੁ ਨ ਜਾਣਈ ਕਰਕ ਕਲੇਜੇ ਮਾਹਿ ॥੧॥

Bholaa Vaidh N Jaanee Karak Kalaejae Maahi ||1||

The foolish physician did not know that the pain was in the mind. ||1||

ਮਲਾਰ ਵਾਰ (ਮਃ ੧) (੩) ਸ. (੧) ੧:੨ - ਗੁਰੂ ਗ੍ਰੰਥ ਸਾਹਿਬ : ਅੰਗ ੧੨੭੯ ਪੰ. ੧੪

Raag Malar Guru Nanak Dev

So, dear friends, whenever our mind is disturbed due to some change in our situation | any kind of loss |attachment |break up | separation |unbearable pain due to some physical ailment; please take help immediately otherwise, we will land up in angry zone where irritability will be our companion and frustration our way of life.

So, hurry up, speak / express yourself / share your concerns/ issues/ problems with someone you trust and who is positive and open too or go to a friend /well wisher /Counselor / Psychologist and get relieved off your baggage.

> *"Venting out your pain areas is of utmost importance to bring peace. Choose any mode; paper-pen, professional, relative, friend but vent out :otherwise you will burst one day."*

Believe me, the hospital admissions would fall and people would live a healthier and longer lives if they are able to win their minds. Let's express ourselves freely without fear of being judged.

Venting/speaking/telling/expressing our concerns, issues, problems, botherations is of urgent importance due to which we have been overthinking a lot... which in turn has someway or other affected our peace of mind, our happiness, our productivity, our presence of mind, our ability to enjoy every moment, capacity to cherish the beauty of blessings God has bestowed upon us.

So, please don't wait.... anymore and please don't let your precious mind cry anymore. Spare some time from whatever you are doing and get your thoughts directed in the direction of positivity and productivity.

No lock is made without a key. Similarly no problem in this beautiful universe is without a solution.

We can persuade on something or let go of a thought only if we talk about it. If we keep things in our mind, we tend to overthink which ultimately blocks our natural energy flow which leads to blockages in different organs-heart/brain etc. Mind is our child and being the parent of such a genius, it's our prime duty to listen to the disturbance of our own mind.

Prolonged stress always.... lead to physical and mental diseases... which forces us to go through painful procedures and be on medication, sometimes life long.

But the good news here is that we can reverse it all.

Even if we start today... listen and understand the misery/ confusion of our mind.... it is healed in no time by giving the right direction to our thoughts.

5. Give energy to progressive thoughts and ignore negative thoughts

Mind is all thoughts, its function is to produce thoughts. From these ever revolving thoughts, we should be wise enough to choose positive ones and ignore the negative ones. Sometimes we get stuck at a particular thought, then we should think of the worst scenario w. r. t. the disturbing thought and let it go. We will be immediately relieved.

All unnecessary thoughts, which has no meaning today should be treated as unwelcome guests. Simply IGNORE them. Ignore means, not to give energy to negative thoughts. Let's understand, Thought has come, we acknowledge, we witness, but we don't get entangled with the thought, we don't start chatting with the thought, we don't start feeling related to the thought. Then what will happen in due course of time is, that particular thought will become weak and vanish.

But on the contrary-what we do is thinking and rethinking about something we have lost in life or some tragedy or some mishappening or some change in situation or change in behaviour of others or unamicable | unexpected behaviour of others, then what happens, mind keep reflecting those thoughts on the screen of our consciousness at small intervals and we start getting irritated| frustrated | aggressive | loud | violent | restlessness because we are giving it power and energy by thinking it again and again. The consequence is we live in pieces not in peace. Mind yearns for something which is not possible in the present and brain forces you to rationalize to the present demands of life. Then its' a clash, which leads to diseases like migraine, depression and dementia. And in most cases, it give rise to illusions; we keep on living in two worlds; divided, crying, devastated and frustrated. We cry for those moments, places, situations or people who have left us or cheated us or made us devastated, for those times which are changed now and those who are with us, we remain agitated with them. Now, when we don't flow with the flow of life, we fail to refresh ourselves.

<u>Myth- Thoughts are our masters, Reality, we being the powerful creation of God, we are the masters of choosing the right thoughts.</u>

Thoughts are creation of our psychological brain- MIND. We have the privilege to give power or snatch power from the thoughts. 'Cause which so ever thought we choose.... will make a pattern and bring similar consequences.

What is assumed to be negative...which is painful, breaking, saddens our mood, make us lifeless, can harm our family, is not healthy for us and our family...

Positive thoughts...which are elevating, ...high goals... unconditional service, usefulness to family and community... being responsible.. patient, polite, tolerant...know how to let go of the things, loving yourself.

If positive thoughts are chosen, it will lead to happy consequences, motivated consequences and if negative chosen, it will lead to sad, depressive consequences;

Once a Dad scoulded son for not getting puncture made for the car despite of 3-4 reminders… a son saw a negative thought.

- 1st thought -Dad always scold me on one one context or other.
- 2nd thought -He doesn't note the good qualities of mine.
- 3rd thought -I am the only one who is always blamed for not accomplishing any task.
- 4th thought - Dad's are not like this.. he is so pricking.
- 5th thought -Actually, my dad doesn't like me
- 6th thought- I am the most unwanted child.

While making this thought pattern again and again, our behaviour becomes irritable, aggressive and frustrated and there's a lot of pain to bear & live with. On the contrary if son could have created this thought at the first place….. that…..

1st thought- I should have done my work at first saying.

2nd thought – I am responsible that is why my dad give me task to do.

3rd thought- My dad really rely upon me for all the matters. After all, I am his productive son.

4th thought- I love my dad very much. He knows how to teach his son to be productive, confident. He knows, responsibility bring confidence and confidence bring productivity.

Now, a positive thought pattern is formed, which instils confidence in son & reflects his behaviour to be healthy, pleasant and attractive.

So, its always our choice to choose right thoughts, so that right thought pattern can be made for constructing a strong, healthy inner personality.

> ***Remember, thoughts can always be created in positive direction.***

6. <u>Get detached from your past thoughts</u>

Remember thoughts never die. Whatever we experience in our lives, each and every thought is registered in our brain. Thoughts keep on moving as per the patterns for example, we see something in our present life, immediately our intelligent brain will bring forward something similar form past in our mind, now it is upto us to get entangled to the past memories or ignore it; just like when some guests visit our home; If we like them, we will cherish their company and if we don't like them, we will ignore them as unwelcome guests. Then unwelcome guests are also intelligent enough not to bother us again as they don't receive any warmth from us.

On the contrary, if we keep on nurturing the thoughts about people or events which had at some point of time thrashed us mercilessly or entertain those people still, we are inviting misery in our life again and again. So we have to learn to forgive and forget those instances, those people and if they still bother we need to divert ourselves to something else. Mind like a child is adamant to distract you again and again on something which you relish but it can be illusion. Some past events or associations which cannot be replayed, something beyond reality, the only way to bring child back to its area of focus is to divert it to something more exciting and fulfilling like if you are sad, rather than sitting and cursing your fate or other people to be the reasons of your sadness rather choose to go for a walk, shopping, movie, holy place, friends place, write a book about your experiences or chat to good people.

Why do we get entangled or become a puppet in the hands of our thoughts, because we relate ourselves with our past experiences very strongly and don't start fresh. One thing must be believed to its truest sense is that everyday we get new opportunity to start our life. It is upto us that we live in the same cocoon/prison of the past or decide to live in the open skies. Remember, past thoughts cannot be removed, but, my friend, I know very well that they can always be replaced with the new ones. Believe me.

> ***ACCEPTING PAST IS THE SOLUTION, NOT ONLY FORGETTING IT. YOU SHOULD KNOW THE REASONS OF YOUR AGONY BUT ACCEPT IT***

Free yourself from thoughts from the past – forgive first then forget

A Story- The Haunted man & his Ghost friend

Once a Professor Richard was haunted with his past life and was very sad because of that. Richard had a best friend who was a ghost. Ghost came up with an idea. Ghost wanted to help professor forget his past by losing his memory. First, Richard was reluctant but then he agreed, when he thought about the pain and aggression he went through each & every moment. Ghost with his magic, help him losing his memory. Richard still went through the moments of emotional pain and misery. Now, his past being erased, he has no hint about the root cause of pain. At times he becomes extremely angry without knowing any reason.

Moral

Unless a person forgives & forgets past all my himself or herself, it is imposible to achieve the peace of mind & soul. Individual by himself or herself alone is responsible for his or her own happiness. If a person decides to forgive & forget, He/she can live a happy life.

7. Accompany productive thoughts

Mind is the powerhouse if properly executed. MIND Is a FLEXIBLE MIRROR. Adjust it to see a better world. Change the perception to change your scene. This is the invisible MAGIC OF PARADIGM SHIFTING and EVERYTHING WOULD CHANGE..... choose the right thought. Thought management plays an important role in shaping our destinies. Many a times, our mind binders don't let us grow and move forward. So, in that case we are like stagnant water which stinks. Start by doing what's necessary, then do what is possible and suddenly you are doing what seemed impossible. Truly said. But no pain no gain. So efforts are needed to be put in effective thinking or no thinking. Either think positive or remain in zero mind. Energy not wasted, so whatever we do, we do with great efficiency and above all, we are not stuck.

IT'S ALL IN THE MIND. MIND IT.

What our personality reflects…the food we eat, the thoughts we entertain…means indulge in …means talk with…means relish.. means enjoy company with …it is not only the company of people outside that makes difference in our life but utmost important is company of thoughts we live with…. we are what our thoughts are…we are what our company is….

very simple…. company of thoughts is more important than the company of physical environment.

There are many examples to support this fact…

1. A teenager relished the company of her cousins who were very good to talk to but were fond of watching movies and shows highlighting lust. Gradually, being in their company for early adolescent years, lust occupied the major space in her life.

2. A young boy accompanied street boys who were gambling, stealing and doing all other dirty clever tasks to earn money. This boy developed all these bad habits at the early stage of his life and after a decade of following these practices of which he was proud of and thereof earning also huge amounts, landed up behind bars in England for 2 decades, his money used in penalty & lawyers fee, family got shattered emotionally, physically and mentally.

3. A lady with empty nest syndrome found herself lonely and depressed, started going to the company of holy people. Few months later, her own home was converted to a temple where God's pious name was being chanted in the morning and evening. Her agony was converted to the bliss of life.

> **Remember, YOU are your Company, choose it thoughtfully and wisely.**

My dear friend, always remember, there are eight pillars of a vibrant mind :

1. **Diet and Nutrition**

   The foundation of mental as well as physical health is diet and nutrition. We must consume wholesome, nutritious food that contains life since we must eat to survive. We should try to be mindful of and appreciative of the food and drink we consume.

   ✓ Make the majority of your meals at home with whole or lightly processed ingredients.

   ✓ The secret to quick, simple meal preparation is to create an eating plan for the week.

   ✓ Pick dishes that include lots of fruits and vegetables.

   ✓ Drink water instead of sugary beverages.

   ✓ Eat more frequent, smaller meals.

2. **Exercise**

   Of course, maintaining a regular exercise routine is crucial for excellent health. It doesn't matter what kind of physical activity you engage in; what matters is that you do something active most days of the week for at least 30 minutes. Whatever activity you choose to undertake, focus on your breathing and let it serve as your compass.

3. **Sleep**

    Consistent, long-term sleep is essential for health. In addition to the fact that sleep is good for our bodies and minds, it also directly affects our level of consciousness. Learn and develop focused habits which can be the key to getting a better night's sleep. Most important is to fix time for your sleep and prepare your surroundings & yourself for a great sound sleep. Chant God's name immediately before falling to deep sleep and thanks Him for bountiful blessings of your life (it may differ from person to person, but definitely, if we are alive, we are blessed with something or other and still keep on striving towards a better life with gratitude).

4. **Blissful early morning**

    Whatever we do early in the morning is going to make impact on the entire day of ours. So, start your day early, before the sun rise with powerful God's name, connecting to the nature and positive loving affirmations to yourself. Believe me, my friend, the whole day, you will find yourself progressive and productive.

5. **Breathe**

    Our physical health and level of stress are significantly impacted by how we breathe. This makes proper breathing a crucial tool for wellness and recovery. Slowing down and deepening our breaths can help us feel less stressed. Our breathing affects our physiology in real time.

6. **Cleansing**

    How crucial is cleansing for a healthy body? The groundwork for a clean, healthy lifestyle impacts us on both the physical and subtle levels. Cleansing is important for the good operation of both the body and the mind, whether you do it regularly (such as with a nasal wash) or more seasonally, say anema (at specific periods of the year from a professional). Keep on learning from the experts in the related field how to maintain a healthy, clean, and bright lifestyle to live a longer life!

And, my pal, where body cleansing is important, it is also vital to keep your surroundings clean and dirt free – especially your toilet seats, toilets, bedrooms, car, office, residence and its'lane.

7. **Mindfulness**

A state of awareness known as mindfulness results from deliberately and non-judgmentally attending to your thoughts in the current moment. It helps us break away from ingrained mental habits rather than trying to repress either happy or bad thoughts. Doing regular yoga elevates mindfulness.

8. **Install anti-virus on mind**

Installing anti-virus on our mind save us from letting in any negativity from the environment to our beautiful minds. Hence our magnetic machines minds, don't get hanged and corrupted.

Conclusion: Learning Mind Management is life saving because if we fail to do so, it can have horrifying consequences.

Our actions, words and thoughts affect every word in the universe. And as we all know, our words and actions are the product of our thoughts. It's as though each victory of good over evil, sanity over insanity, life over death, love over lust, selfless acts of love over selfishness: means a collective victory and brings about cumulative joy and happiness.

We do talk of distractions, we talk of stability, we even talk of life skills, but precisely why don't we talk about our thoughts in depth. Why don't we often talk about thinking skills. It ought to be talked of because its' the thoughts which are governing us, which are designing our destiny. We keep saying to everyone;stay in present, live in present. But the thoughts which has been registered in our sub-conscious mind /blind self …keep on haunting us and we start chasing them or talking to them; which results in our misfortunes, unhappiness, disturbance of mind, depression and anxieties.

Many a times we keep on nurturing our so called pleasant or most precious thoughts that they become an integral part of our being.

In this scenario, we are divided. Partially we are living with these thoughts and partially with the present. In the present also, when something unpleasant/unwelcoming turns on /we switch over/escape to our so called pleasant memories/thoughts. Hence, we are not living in peace, we are living in pieces.

If we are able to channelize our thoughts well, if we are able to learn these skills at a very early age, then we will be more focussed and we could easily get away with our distractions. Parents and teachers can play a very important role here if they are true listeners in the real sense. If we can do this, we can save people especially youth from many mental illnesses and emotional setbacks. We can produce awakened society. We can help people live life to their fullest.

In my research project on Effective Parenting, I guided parents to give wisdom to their teens on thoughts. We have been doing it during Parenting Seminars since last 2 decades. We are approaching youngsters in schools and colleges to save humanity from being absent minded.

Here, the most pathetic group is the middle aged and old women. Ladies who cross 40 years of age are struggling with their minds to come out of their past images/past thoughts/past crushes/past lifestyles/past power positions. But unfortunately, over the years /decades; they have made these thoughts so favourite of theirs, that they have formed 80% of their lives around these illusions. These are actually fantasies/illusions, which does not exist in present.

In present, whatever blessings they have been showered with, they are unable to see and enjoy. As professionals in the field, we do counsel such aggrieved persons, but my concern is to approach them at an early age, when they are being trapped by these thoughts.

Real life Case studies

I. A case of eighty years old woman who still operates from her power position which she used to enjoy when she was forty and enjoy her social life with her married daughters without considering the importance of opinions and consent of her sixty year old son and his spouse who are her guardians in the present scenario. She ends up breaking her son's family and her daughter-in-law warm attachment with her sister-in-laws and their children.

II. A case of nice woman who had seen her mother with her boy friend, repel physical intimacy with her loving husband.

III. A case of middle aged woman who still nurtured memories of her lover was living in pieces so she developed guilt of cheating, fear of being caught, regret for her life and unhappiness.

IV. A case of an adult male who get panic attacks on nurturing repeated toxic thoughts about his childhood experiences. He had 4-5 memories where his parents physically abused him. He recalled it again and again and developed mental ailment.

V. A case of teenage girl who get anxiety attacks on overthinking about parental conflicts. Husband and wife fights frequently….. this left bitter memories on her mind. She thought it again and again and got severe panic attacks.

VI. A case study of teenager who has nurtured fear feelings about her step father who sexually harassed her by touching in one way or another on her private parts.

VII. A case of 65 years old woman who wants her total instructional power control over the children and household. She becomes puppet in the hands of her daughter who motivates her to do it hence spoils her amicable relation with the family of her son where she has lived in her lifetime.

I'm not saying that we can take all misery from the planet, but still I'm convinced that if we can channelize these wandering thoughts well on time, we can save many broken hearts.

Because mishappenings related to relationships take place due to the distorted /unchannelised thought patterns. Our guides, parents and teachers also need to be enlightened on the subject because young minds are looking on to them for support and help in the times of turmoil and confusion but alas they are least equipped to give proper guidance.

IT'S ALL IN THE MIND. MIND IT

Your task is to only

1. Focus on the present priorities

2. Quality of your thoughts

3. Self improvement--Excercise, taking balanced Diet, meditation, living in non reactive mode

4. Building the new not repairing the old

5. Believing in yourself.

6. Leave your past behind whatsoever.

You just focus on giving on the right thing to the world. Because Universal Law is; "whatever You give to the universe it has to come back to you". So, give love, appreciation, encouraging words, healing words, smiles, uplifting words inspite of the fact......that the other person deserves it or not because you are not giving it according to other person but you are giving because you only want these to come back.... & gradually you only are filled with Love, Compassion, smiles, encouragement & then you don't have to force to give these to anyone... you will AUTOMATICALLY spread because you only have these.

> *Befriend with your own mind and win it to support you in your positive thinking and make your life a celebration.*

Positive thoughts...which are elevating, ...high goals... unconditional service, usefulness to family and community... being responsible.. patient -polite- tolerant...know how to let go of the things and on the top love yourself.

Chapter 3

Understanding Dis-ease and Being at Ease

<u>**"Be easy with yourself at the right time, otherwise you are ought to get dis-eased."**</u>

— We often ask each other, hey buddy how is your health and the most common reply is I'm fine; apart from small disease here & there. This so called small disease is only manifested into a big health hazard if ignored in its budding stage. Let's try to understand your dis-ease. It means you are not at ease with yourself and on the bigger front, you are not at ease with your life. You are not living, you are only surviving. In most of the cases you are living somebody's else life as conditioned upon you. Your real self is buried under so many layers of the world's expectations of yours from your worldly role, that your soul wants to breathe, your soul wants to be heard. At the bottom of your core existence, You want to live life on your own terms & choices but you have stopped expressing yourself due to fear of unacceptance or in the effort of making your near & dear ones' happy. Your own happiness in all this endeavour has been hided underneath. This mental agony is manifested into physical diseases in the form of migraines, ulcers, allergies, cancer etc. for which you start taking medicines and keep on consulting specialists. Though very important to do so, the utmost emergency here is to find the root cause of your mental disturbance.

— What is there in life, which is bothering you. There must be some underlying root cause. Vent out your problems now, otherwise, it will burst as a volcano in the form of a disease/or at the wrong time.

— If you want to lead a life with ease, it is important to be happy. What are you doing to be happy and spread happiness in the world is a big question ? Are all your cherished dreams fulfilled. Why our dreams not always fulfilled? Because we compromise. We give up to the judgements of small minds. In order to make someone else happy on non-productive things, we sacrifice our own happiness.

— Unresolved issues from the past, which are still hanging on in your life without making peace, are mostly the biggest reason for our agony. Resolve them today by stepping into the past a little and open communication.

— Remember ! You can't please everybody. You cannot even justify to everybody. Everybody has their own level of survival. Some survive as ducks but eagle feel suffocated among ducks. Everyone has their own ideology. Love their ideology and yours too.

— And It doesn't mean that you are selfish or not considerate, it means that you are compassionate. You want to live your life happily & hence make the life of the people around you very exciting. For this, you have to make your relation with yourself very sincere & healthy.

- Nobody can ever feel the pain you are going through. So, you only have to express and give shape to your dreams & choices. If you don't face your fear & chase your dream you will be duck who is always complaining about blessed life as the toughest one. Moreover, you will keep on living the pain.

- Some people live in fear. Some people conquer the fear. We cannot fully meet the expectation of others, meet the ideology of people around us, inspite of doing every effort to please them. So, love your own uniqueness & wisdom. Have faith on God. Do your duties. Don't tolerate what your soul can't take.

- Those who dare to conquer the fear have to walk through their own insecurities with grace. Stop expecting that everyone will understand you. You need to express yourself. Initially, your near & dear ones may feel bad but those who surely love you and are concerned about you; when they see you happy, they will also be happy and those who don't love you, how does it matter.

- Stop diminishing yourself. When you are responsible, right & courteous, don't fear anything. There is no fear that can't be conquered. Let your voice be heard. Why afraid to Love? Love All. But love yourself first. Think first yourself then others, because "if I'm happy I'll be able to keep others happy".

- Don' t disturb yourself for the judgements, opinions, thoughts of people. Smile to them, forget their thoughts, follow your own paths with your own thoughts & ideas. Don't judge people and don't get involved into judgements of others.

- <u>**Loss in life**</u>

- Every human life is going to experience loss in life. The loss of a thing or a person very dear to your heart, whom you love dearly, irrespective of the fact that other person loves you with that intensity or not but you have nurtured his/her love and love his/ her company and closeness as ecstasy and when you lose such a relationship due to any reasons in this universe, your entire world is shattered. Then, work on yourself to accept the truth along with wishing best of the best for your lost lovely relationships in prayers. Don't curse anyone for LEAVING YOU because God has seen good in that way only. He/she has only acted his/her role in it.

- God knows it was not for you anymore, but see, still wonders of God are abundant. 'Don't CRY.' If one thing is taken back from you in any way as per the universal call, believe me, being God's favourite, He knows that you deserve the best. The lost relation is not meant to add any further value to your magnificient life, that's why it is not with you today. It's absolutely OK fine, perfect. Because to compensate with it, God will definitely bestow you with His choicest blessings one by one in many shades and colours;so that you don't miss or focus on the loss and focus your energies on the abundant blessings of God and REJOICE.

- Acceptance is peace of mind. Life is not dependent on one event or one relationship / take learning from your sad situation & move ahead. Be in gratitude for abundant blessings of your life. Write all your blessings on a paper and say from core of your heart, THANKU GOD.

- **<u>Holy Sri Guru Granth Sahib Ji, Ang 268</u>**

  ਦਸ ਬਸਤੁ ਲੇ ਪਾਛੈ ਪਾਵੈ ॥

  दस बसतू ले पाछै पावै ॥

  Das bastū le pāchhai pāvai.

  ਏਕ ਬਸਤੁ ਕਾਰਨਿ ਬਿਖੋਟਿ ਗਵਾਵੈ ॥

  एक बसतु कारनि बिखोटि गवावै ॥

  Ėk basat kāran bikhot gavāvai.

  He obtains ten things, and puts them behind him;

  for the sake of one thing withheld, he forfeits his faith.

  But what if that one thing were not given, and the ten were taken away?

  Then, what could the fool say or do?

- All experiences of life are guiding you towards your destiny(especially the most bitter & painful experiences). God wants you to go through that pain to make you experienced to relieve pain of the humanity. "A candle cannot light other candles without being burnt herself". So every worthwhile contributor has to go through pain – just see the most talented doctors and surgeons who instill new life in you. They have gone through the pain of studying big books, understanding the concepts in depth and little detail of pain causing ailments. Similarly, if anybody who is going through pain and losses in life -we must understand that he is being trained for a big cause of healing the humanity simply because when you are in pain you try every method of healing it, with which later, you can save many others.

– **<u>Holy Sri Guru Granth Sahib Ji, Ang 282, 283</u>**

ਮਨ ਮੁਰਖ ਕਾਹੇ ਬਿਲਲਾਈਐ ॥

मन मूरख काहे बिलिलाईऐ ॥

Man mūrakẖ kāhe billā¤ī¤ai.

ਪੁਰਬ ਲਿਖੇ ਕਾ ਲਖਿਆ ਪਾਈਐ ॥

पुरब लखि का लखिआ पाईऐ ॥

Purab likẖe kā likẖi¤ā pā¤ī¤ai.

O foolish mind, why do you cry and bewail?

 You shall obtain your pre-ordained destiny.

God is the Giver of pain and pleasure.

Abandon others, and think of Him alone.

Whatever He does - take comfort in that.

Why do you wander around, you ignorant fool?

What things did you bring with you?

You cling to worldly pleasures like a greedy moth.

Dwell upon the Lord's Name in your heart.

Thus you shall return to your home with honor.

<u>Victor from Victim</u>

– There's an inner power that makes winners or losers and the winners are the ones who really listen to the truth of their hearts no matter who they are, no matter what they did, no matter where they've come from, they can always become a better version of themselves. The victor draws strength from troubles, smiles during distress and grows stronger with prayers and hope. He/She always say " I am one of them "-I am the victor not the victim of my circumstances.

> **'Be willing to surrender what you are, for what you could become in your life'**

Direction is more important than speed. This is winning. Winning with strengths & over powering weakness.

Today, almost everyone is suffering in the hands of his/her own thoughts. (In further reading, mostly you will find only masculine gender to denote both the genders). The most rich, the most wise and most educated men are the victims of restlessness and anger. In spite of having abundant comforts, man is not happy. Nobody is responsible for this misery; still, everywhere BLAME GAME is speculated. Everyone is searching happiness outside. Man is searching for happiness in just everything whatever can be bought by money. Shopping in Malls, watching movies, shows on Netflix, rides in luxury cars, eating rich food etc. These activities, no doubt, give instant temporary excitement. Once out of this momentary pleasure, life is same; not less than hell sometimes- relationship issues, ego hassles, attachment entanglements, problems in day to day transactional analysis, still others; stress at work, inobedient children and non-understanding spouse at home, financial crunch, unrealistic luring goals, heart breaking regrets and grudges, stiff face with divorced smile, lack of time and energy, back to back meetings and as a result no peace and contentment. Life, such a magnificent life is passing without any bliss and celebration and will be lost without making any difference to the self, of course, indirectly to the magical world.

Then the question arises, we visited this wonderful planet 'Earth' and went back to our origin- eating, cribbing, sleeping, gossiping and superficially merrying also. That's the end of our story. Let's reflect upon this philosophy - whenever we go to a friends' or relatives' place, we take something as a gift for them. Yes!. Yes, then point to consider here is when we have been given the opportunity to be with our family, colleagues, internal and external customers in our life, what is our contribution in their life, what difference are we making in transforming their life to be happier, more meaningful and constructive, which cherished moments are we presenting to those around us, which soft skills are we using in all our relations to make them blissful.

Our happiness is ultimately the most expensive gift for everyone around us. But it is stolen by our own negative thoughts. The thief is inside us which needs to be caught at the right time before it steals our peace, happiness and dignity. Thief needs to be thrown out and our real home, our powerful and smart minds needs to be decorated with positive thoughts.

The simple self introspective questions are;

1. How can I give happiness to anyone when I myself is not happy?

2. How can I give something to someone which I am not having myself?

Stress is commonly used word today in everyone's vocabulary irrespective of gender, age and profession. Many stress relieving centers and institutes are opened in the present era. Of course, they are doing their job nicely. Many people are also consulting psychiatrists, psychologists and professional counselors to get rid of the misery they are living with.

Changing Situations

- ***Choose one of your stress causes.*** How can this situation be changed or improved? For example:
- ***Relationship stress*** - assertive communication training, setting boundaries, resolving conflict
- ***Overcommitment*** - setting boundaries, saying no, eliminating some things from your schedule
- ***Grief and loss*** - seeking support, journaling, finding enjoyable activities to fill your day

Developing Effective Coping Strategies

- It is important to use a variety of coping strategies to manage stress that inevitably will occur. By regularly practicing coping strategies, you can stop stress from building up and prevent stress overload.
- Not all stressful situations are within our control, and not every situation can be changed. Effective, healthy coping skills can allow you to get through difficult times.
- ***Examples of healthy coping strategies:***
- ***- be busy-v. important***
- - learn relaxation techniques
- - journalise your thoughts
- - do deep breathing
- - exercise daily

As you find, in this book, there are many true cases and success stories from victim to victor, it has been proved that we are miserable not because of insufficient comforts of life or because of people or situations but because of our unchannelized negative thoughts. We unknowingly operate under long term conditioned mind. We are cherishing either negative thoughts or negative people. Our conditioned subconscious mind give valid reasons to our conscious mind very cleverly for doing the same. This is why we are not able to come out of our misery.

Our greatest self has been waiting our whole life, so, let's not make it wait any longer. Its' perfectly okay to make mistakes, to have bad days, to be less than perfect, to do what's best for you, to be yourself; but now at this time of your life, you need to act smart, simple and stable by applying soft skills in all your relations, in all areas of your life.

Its' not the mountain we conquer but ourselves (Sir Edmund Hillary). We all make mistakes, have struggles, and even regret things in our past. But we are not our mistakes, we are not our struggles and we have all the power to shape our day and our future.

> *There is no substitute for Hardwork and Purity. Put efforts to change your thoughts, perception and life. Life is not about having all you want, it's about appreciating all that you have. "To fail means you have tried, to hurt means you have loved and to survive means you have learned."*

Top 5 Guidelines for Success, NOW

> *— I strongly urge you to take the following 5 measures in order to make this year -YOUR year in the spirit of joyful service centered around your highest values.*

- #1: **Make a note of the one project that you must do without fail.**

- Your Mighty Mission for the current year is this. Forget about trying to influence 100 different things. **Just create one true masterpiece**, and wonderful benefits will flow.

- #2: **List your top five principles for living.**

- When you work and live according to your own terms and standards, you'll be content and extremely productive.

- #3: **Decide on your top three priorities for each of the major facets of your life (personal development, family, career, finances, fitness, spirituality, etc.).**

- #4. **In order to reverse-engineer the current year as your ideal year, create ten deliverables for each three-month period as you build up each quarter of this year.**

- #5: **Schedule time slots on your monthly calendar for your deliverables and action activities.**

- Please dedicate a full day to doing this in solitude. Your performance during the current year will demonstrate the value of your work.

- Remember MY DEAR,

- Every good thought contribute its share to the ultimate result of our life. We may find the worst enemy or best friend in ourself. We will never be alone if we are accompanied by noble thoughts. Headache, migraine won't go or ease will not come unless or until we start following right thoughts and right code of conduct as per God's teachings. Keep God on your side…. get peace …control your thoughts…

redirect your thoughts…. as per holy wisdom and live free in this life.

Holy Sri Guru Granth Sahib Ji, Ang 270

ਮਨ ਤਿਸੁ ਸਿਮਰਤ ਕਿਉ ਆਲਸੁ ਕੀਜੈ ॥

मन तिसु सिमरत किउ आलसु कीजै ॥

Man ṯis simraṯ ki▫o ālas kījai.

ਮਨ ਤਿਸੁ ਪ੍ਰਭ ਕਉ ਕਬਹੁ ਨ ਬਿਸਾਰੀ ॥

मन तिसु प्रभ कउ कबहू न बिसारी ॥

Man ṯis parabẖ ka▫o kabhū na bisārī.

O mind, why are you so lazy?

Why don't you remember Him in meditation?

O mind, never forget that God.

By His Grace, you have land, gardens and wealth;

keep God enshrined in your heart.

O mind, the One who formed your form -

Meditate on Him - the One Invisible Lord;

By His Grace, your hands move and work.

By His Grace, you obtain the supreme status.

Why forsake God, and attach yourself to another?

So, my dear friends and book mates, be at ease with yourself. Love and respect yourself for being the lovely creature of Lord Almighty and thereafter love each and every creature produced by the SUPER POWER. And foremost, always keep God on your side by following His path.

Chapter 4

Save Yourself from Emotional Traps and Live at Ease

Holy Sri Guru Granth Sahib Ji, Ang 70, 71 and 72

ਇਹ ਜਗਿ ਮੀਤੁ ਨ ਦੇਖਿਓ ਕੋਈ ॥

इह जगि मीतु न देखिओ कोई ॥

Ih jag mīt na dekhiᵃo koᵃī.

ਸਗਲ ਜਗਤੁ ਅਪਨੈ ਸੁਖਿ ਲਾਗਿਓ ਦੁਖ ਮੈ ਸੰਗਿ ਨ ਹੋਈ ॥੧॥ ਰਹਾਉ ॥

सगल जगतु अपनै सुखि लागिओ दुख मै संगि न होई ॥१॥ रहाउ ॥

Sagal jagat apnai sukh lāgiᵃo dukh mai sang na hoᵃī. ||1|| rahāᵃo.

In this world, I have not found any true friend.

The whole world is attached to its own pleasures, and when trouble comes, no one is with you. ||1|| Pause||

"What is life?"

Is it a cry or a smile.

I wanna raise this question to God,

Why've you send us from heaven to the world …so cold

Sometimes I wonder where to spend life,

When everywhere there is prevailing cry and crime.

Oh God! There is request of your little child,

Take in your lap to protect me from the people –So wild.

Either take me or change the people,

Hearts which don't even know what is love.

Oh my dear lord please do mend the world,

or it would be hard to bear this even for the bold.

Just cultivate the seed of love in the hearts of people,

Good Heavens! This world would be then place to be lived.

Do analyse and act accordingly my friend,

Put a frog into a vessel filled with water and start heating the water. As a temperature of water begin to rise, the frog adjusts its' body temperature accordingly. The frog keep on adjusting its' body temperature with the increasing temperature of water. When the water is about to reach to boiling point, the frog cannot adjust anymore. At this point, The frog decided to jump out. The frog tried to jump but its unable to do so because it has lost whole of its strength in adjusting with the rising water temperature. Very soon the frog dies. So, what killed the frog? Think about it. I know many of us will say the boiling water but the truth about what killed the frog was its inability to decide when to jump out. The same scenario happens with us while facing the adversities of life, but we need to be sure when we need to adjust and when we need to move on. There are times when we need to face situation and take appropriate actions. If we allow people to exploit us physically, emotionally, financially, spiritually, mentally they will continue to do so, timely we need to decide when to jump, when we still have the strength to do so. Now, let's understand it by an example of a girl named ***Alina.***

Alina's life ideology was Love Begets Love

Granny told me when I was a kid, my dear love, You'll find this is the world full of love.

I was brought up with these words, ringing in my ears, "my love! Love begets love".

Then came the stage, I grew up to that age dreaming about that lovely love.

Whole life was gone, searching for love but found nothing of that sort called love.

Everyone played with my toy called love and the return gift was my broken heart…. Heart filled with love. Frustrated and annoyed, I asked my granny residing in the heaven …. Where would I beget Love.

Came the reply…. How silly, in the world full of hatred my Love… You won't beget Love.

A Real Story-

Alina, a darling daughter of elite class parents. She was brought up with lots of love, care, high class luxuries and good education. This girl, though intelligent and smart was very innocent. She believed this world to be a very nice and friendly place.

No doubt, she was liberal. But as envisaged by her lovely eyes, this world is not that same. Roses does not bloom without thorns. Positives compliment the negatives. Good accompanies the bad and among the angels like her, exist the devils. If I define devils here, so I would say those beings who are enslaved by the biggest invisible powers in this universe; and these powers are ego, anger, lust, greed, fear and attachment. According to my understanding, these powers put us in the intention zone of grabbing, possessing, expecting and snatching. These devils play their role better than the angels because they are more determined towards achieving their goals. So, often angels realize their trap very late and in this process they have to pay a big cost in being associated with them.

Alina, too paid a heavy cost. When her hormones were playing havoc on her during her youthful years of onset of puberty, she came across a brother of her best friend who played dirty emotional game with her. This brother was in a hunt for trapping female's love to use her for his sexual gratification. With his clever moves, he was somehow successful which brought pain, agony and misery in Alina's life. She could not timely decide to jump out of the emotional trap created by him and suffered for a long time.

So, below is the cry of Alina, which she expressed like this;

<u>No Humanity</u>

Just wanna write something on a paper.
Something about my hurts 'n' my pains.
Of course! Given by those who were loved the most,
unable to understand aren't they really ghosts.
Oh God ! your human hearts are such complications,
one forgets oneself to please the loved ones.
Then that day comes, they don't even recognize you,
Simply laughs and say, Hey! You were foolish 'n' we've used you.
Inside broken weeps tender heart,

Alas! How can it get it in the world with no humanity.

> **But, always remember, among the devils only exist the angels. In this world exist the positive and truthful people, where in majority you find deceiving souls. But this is only possible with God's grace.**

Holy Sri Guru Granth Sahib Ji, Ang 779

ਠਾਕੁਰ ਭਾਣੀ ਸਾ ਗੁਣਵੰਤੀ ਤਿਨ ਹੀ ਸਭ ਰੰਗ ਮਾਣਾ ॥

ठाकुर भाणी सा गुणवंती तिन ही सभ रंग माणा ॥

Ṯẖākur bẖāṇī sā guṇvanṯī ṯin hī sabẖ rang māṇā.

She alone is virtuous, who is pleasing to her Lord and Master. She alone enjoys all the pleasures.

Angel among common

Oh my God ! Give me that strength to face the world beyond the length,

Where no body is no one's; where I find just hypocrits.

Everybody has so many colours changing like the hues of sky above.

Can't anyone be my own. On whom I can rely upon.

A single person but faithful, just want such an angel.

He who makes me feel in so many ways, that he'll be there in my rainy days.

Whose helping hand I could hold, to protect me from the roaring stroms.

But such a person is difficult to find 'cause just angels are of such kind.

Still, if someone finds such a person, he/she has really got the world.

> *Outer beauty may allure you instantly but inner beauty gives you the warmth you cannot live without. Pray God to bestow you association with such angels only and also put us in the same category too. Then you have got everything in this world.*

My friend, I feel touched everytime I read this letter AND I really want this to be read by every child, parent and a teacher. Lincoln was the 16th president of the United States and one of the great American leaders. His letter to his son's teacher, MUST READ BY ALL OF YOU;

<u>It give us an important insight to be smart still humble, innocent still clever.</u>

He will have to learn,
I know,
That all men are not just (fair),
All men are not true.
But teach him also that
For every scoundrel
(Dishonest) there is a hero;
That for every selfish politician,

There is a dedicated leader...
Teach him for every enemy there is a friend.
Steer him away from envy,
If you can teach him
the secret of quiet laughter.

Let him learn early that the bullies are the easiest to lick.....
Teach him, if you can, the wonder of books..... But also give him
quite time to ponder the enternal mystery of birds in the sky bees
in the sun, and the flowers on the green hillside.

In the school teach him
It is for honorable to fall than to chest.....
Teach him to have faith in his own ideas,
Even if everyone tells him they are wrong...
Teach him to be gentle with gentle people,
And tough with the tough.
Try to give my son

The strength not to follow the crowd when everyone is getting
on the band wagon.... Teach him to listen to all men.... But teach
him also to filter all he hears on the screen of truth, and take only
the good that come through.

Teach him to close his ears to howling mob and to stand and
fight if he think he is right.

Treat him gently,
But not to cuddle him,
Because only the test of fire makes fine still steel.
Let him have a courage to be impatient...
Let him have the patience to be brave.

Teach him always to have sublime faith in himself,
Because then he will have subline faith in mankind.
Teach him if you can,
How to laugh when he is sad...

Teach him there is no shame in tears, teach him to ridicule at cynics

And to beware of too much sweetness..... Teach him to sell his strength and brain to the highest bidders but never to put price tag on his heart and soul.

> ***Beware of Emotional Traps;***
>
> ***We are emotionally trapped mostly because of Delusion in love. So, Beware.***

Holy Sri Guru Granth Sahib Ji, Ang 268

ਬਟਾਉ ਸਿਉ ਜੋ ਲਾਵੈ ਨੇਹ ॥

बटाऊ सिउ जो लावै नेह ॥

Batāᵁū siᵁo jo lāvai neh.

ਤਾ ਕਉ ਹਾਥਿ ਨ ਆਵੈ ਕੇਹ ॥

ता कउ हाथि न आवै केह ॥

Ŧā kaᵁo hāth na āvai keh.

One who gives her love to a passing traveler -nothing shall come into her hands in this way.

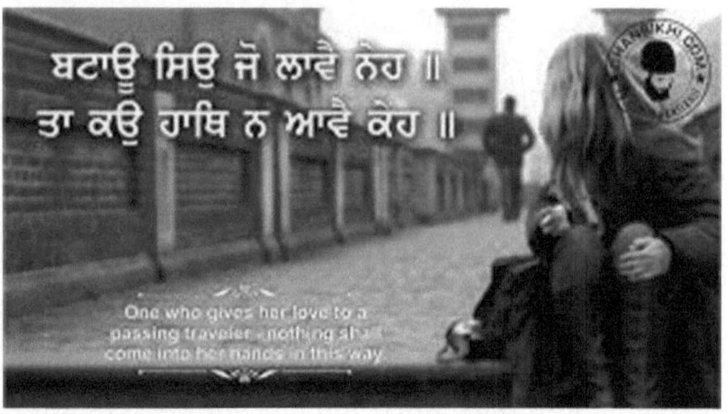

Beware of emotional traps. Be your own bestfriend…

"We have to learn to be our best friend because we fall too easily into the trap of being our own worst enemies"

You have the power………

But the question is how long shall the pain stay in you. Pain is getting trapped in the thoughts and emotions which have no meaning today. Pain is in the same old habits, in the same old belief patterns, in same old perceptions. One day, we need to win over the pain of attachment, duality, possession, greed, lust and ego. If we continue doing the same, we will be in ignorance, we will live in ignorance and die in ignorance, again taking rebirth in ignorance, it is like we have never taken admission in the nursery class of enlightenment, doing Ph. D. is a far off thing. So in the next birth again on the basis of Karma, our admission is not guaranted in the school of shedding ignorance and getting enlightenment.

Holy Sri Guru Granth Sahib Ji, Ang 283

ਅਬਿਨਾਸੀ ਪਰਭੁ ਮਨ ਮਹਿ ਰਾਖੁ ॥

अबिनासी प्रभु मन महि राखु ॥

Abẖināsī parabẖ man mėh rākẖ.

ਮਾਨੁਖ ਕੀ ਤੂ ਪਰੀਤਿ ਤਿਆਗੁ ॥

ਮਾਨੁਖ ਕੀ ਤੂ ਪ੍ਰੀਤਿ ਤਿਆਗੁ ॥

Mānukẖ kī ṯū parīṯ ṯiⁿāg.

Keep the Immortal Lord God enshrined within your mind.

Renounce your love and attachment to people.

Beyond Him, there is nothing at all.

The One Lord is pervading among all.

Delusion in love

Love can be a powerful and destabilizing experience. People often experience it as not wholly pleasant. You could say that ideas of love are fundamentally delusional because the beliefs associated with love just don't correspond with reality.

ਜੋ ਦੀਸੈ ਸੋ ਵਿਨਸਨਾ ਮਨ ਕੀ ਮਤਿ ਤਿਆਗੁ ॥੧॥ ਰਹਾਉ ॥

Jo Dheesai So Vinasanaa Man Kee Math Thiaag ||1|| Rehaao ||

Whatever is seen, shall pass away. Abandon the intellectualizations of your mind. ||1||Pause||

ਸਿਰੀਰਾਗੁ (ਮਃ ੫) (੪੧) ੧:੨ - ਗੁਰੂ ਗਰੰਥ ਸਾਹਿਬ : ਅੰਗ ੫੦ ਪੰ. ੫

Sri Raag Guru Arjan Dev

If it seems difficult, pray whole heartedly to dear God. He will bestow His help to you at all places and protect you from the design of your enemies.

ਖੜਗਕੇਤੁ ਮੈ ਸਰਨਿ ਤਿਹਾਰੀ ॥ਆਪੁ ਹਾਥ ਦੈ ਲੇਹੁ ਉਬਾਰੀ ॥ ਸਰਬ ਠੌਰ ਮੋ ਹੋਹੁ ਸਹਾਈ ॥ਦੁਸਟ ਦੋਖ ਤੇ ਲੇਹੁ ਬਚਾਈ ॥੪੦੧॥ (Holy Sri Dasham Granth, Chaupayi Sahib), which means, bestow thy help own me at all places protect me from the design of my enemies. 401.

Reminding Again, Befriend God.

Holy Sri Guru Granth Sahib Ji, Ang 281

ਤਜਹੁ ਸਿਆਨਪ ਸੁਰਿ ਜਨਹੁ ਸਿਮਰਹੁ ਹਰਿ ਹਰਿ ਰਾਇ ॥

तजहु सिआनप सुरि जनहु सिमरहु हरि हरि राइ ॥

Ŧajahu si◌ānap sur janhu simrahu har har rā◌e.

ਏਕ ਆਸ ਹਰਿ ਮਨਿ ਰਖਹੁ ਨਾਨਕ ਦੁਖੁ ਭਰਮੁ ਭਉ ਜਾਇ ॥੧॥

एक आस हरि मनि रखहु नानक दूखु भरमु भउ जाइ ॥१॥

Ėk ās har man rakhahu Nānak ḏūkh bharam bha◌o jā◌e. ||1||

Give up your cleverness, good people - remember the Lord God, your King! Enshrine in your heart, your hopes in the One Lord. O Nanak, your pain, doubt and fear shall depart. ||1||

God condemns the people who do evil deeds, are corrupted and are not helpful to others. So, don't worry, He Himself will decide how to bring them on right path as per God's will. Trust God.

Holy Sri Guru Granth Sahib Ji, Ang 269

ਮਿਥਿਆ ਚਰਨ ਪਰ ਬਿਕਾਰ ਕਉ ਧਾਵਹਿ ॥

मिथिआ चरन पर बिकार कउ धावहि ॥

Mithi◌ā charan par bikār ka◌o ḏhāvėh.

ਮਿਥਿਆ ਮਨ ਪਰ ਲੋਭ ਲੁਭਾਵਹਿ ॥

मिथिआ मन पर लोभ लुभावहि ॥

Mithi◌ā man par lobh lubhāvėh.

False are the feet which run to do evil to others.

False is the mind which covets the wealth of others.

False is the body which does not do good to others.

He says one thing, and does something else.

There is no love in his heart, and yet with his mouth he talks tall.

The Omniscient Lord God is the Knower of all.

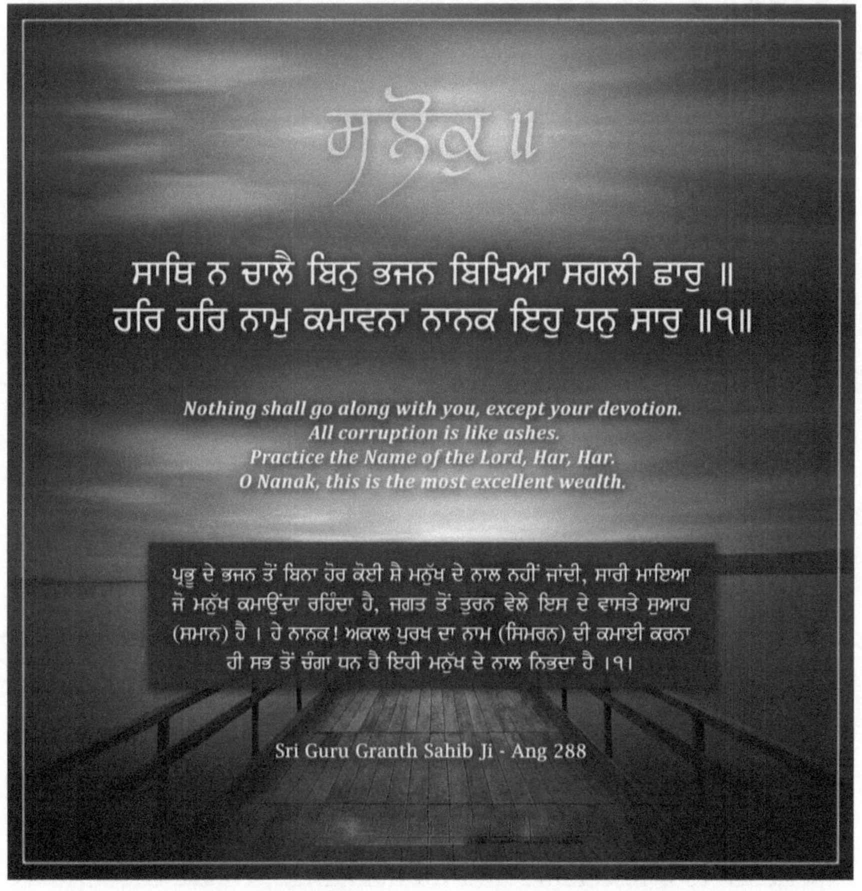

Chapter 5

The Couple, Sex and Marriage

The Couple

Much of the anguish and the elation in our lives begins with a glance, a kiss and then—a lifelong struggle to make sense of the verb *to love*. Patients have faith that their doctor can set a broken bone or offer pills to adjust their blood pressure. But poets, philosophers and psychologists alike have long seen love as intangible and nebulous, beyond our abilities to define. In my experience as a researcher and humanitarian, I have encountered many, many people trying to tackle that puzzle. Countless times I have heard: "I don't know what went wrong with my relationship and I have no idea how to put it right. "

We have two couples waiting to be introduced to you, one is Jacob Peterson & Lilly Peterson living in Brooklyn, NewYork,

U. S. A. Jacob is working in a multinational company. Lilly is working in Rogers Telecommunications as Head of Credit card Department. They are in live-in relationship for last 5 years now.

Morning scene at their residence in New York. Lilly worried about Jacob coming home late at night as he might had one night stand yesterday and if asked he would have confessed that it was only a small fling and he didn't want her to act like a wife. Jacob is sleeping and dreaming about her new girlfriend with whom he spent his last night. Lilly and Jacob has many psychological issues to address for this relationship on personal grounds- Trust, Honesty, Integrity, Loyality, Threat of STDs and Belongingness.

Another family, Tony & Priya, living in the lush green hilly area of Amb, district Una, Himachal Pradesh, India. Tony is working as a Cashier in Bank of Una located on the Una road, 3 kms. from their humble but lovely residence. Priya is a homemaker doing distance education course in Home -Science. They are a happily married couple.

Morning scene at Tony's home- Priya preparing breakfast in the kitchen and Tony holds her in his arms from the back and he tightens his grip on her, she bubbles with infinite love. With butterflies in their stomach both end up in their bedroom merged into one another. Tony and Priya don't have any psychological issue to address for this beautiful committed relationship of theirs'. They believe that Trust, Honesty, Integrity, Loyality and Belongingness are the very foundation of this holy knot.

The Couple have multiple unspoken promises to live by for which they are committed to each other. To quote the few vows, which naturally need to be administered by the couple, once you are a couple are being;

a mersimerising lover,

being all ears listener,

being committed,

being the biggest praiser of your partner,

being the motivational trainer for your partner,

being the better half,

being the grace,

being the most cherished blessing,

being the secret sharing friend,

being the body guard,

being the psychologist,

being the most caring nurse,

being the volunteering helper,

being the healer,

being the saint for salvation,

being the personal coach,

being the air you breathe,

being the mind you think,

being the soul on journey

AND, we can all analyse & BRAIN STORM that it is only possible to adhere to all these beautiful and unspoken promises in the commitment as a couple in whole hearted holy bond of marriage.

> *Sex is a physical activity and making love to someone you love is meditation. It is pure & pious. Keep control over your mind to save your precious virginity for the love of your life. And if you are illusioned that you have got one, don't rush for physical intimacy before a holy marital knot, otherwise you will end up losing all the peace and beauty of this magnificient life.*

The Couple in a romantic relationship without marriage

It is assumed to be trendy today worldwide to stay together as a couple without getting married. Physical intimacy is of course very important in a relationship and a couple needs to be very active physically. But there is the right time for everything in a relationship. There is always a risk of being duped in a relationship before tying the knot, and sex before marriage can worsen the situation. Looks very rosy and exciting during the initial phase but as the studies on mental health, psycho social societal structures and live real life stories reveals that entering into romantic relationship without the commitment brings in a high level of insecurity, lack of feeling of belongingness, lack of trust in the relationship, threat for the female to get pregnant, lack of acceptance in the society, low self esteem and lack of fulfilment in the relationship which leads to many unforeseen conflicts, chaos and enraged relationships in the later part of this set up. Moreover, it is considered as a sin in many holy books.

Faith has a lot to say about what boundaries you should set regarding physical intimacy in love before marriage. After being so connected to the partner emotionally and physically, it can be stressful to go through everything, if the relationship does not work out. It is the biggest reason you should not have sex before marriage and you must understand your boundaries. Getting attracted to someone and loving him /her too much is very natural and heavenly but breaking boundaries and surrendering yourself to your lover before the commitment can be life torturing experience for you later which may lead to chronic depression, anxiety, wrong decisions and bring a hard time for you and your family. So beware to fall and wait for the holy bond before getting emotionally and physically tied up. And if your mind doesn't listen to you, make it understand through Holy wisdom.

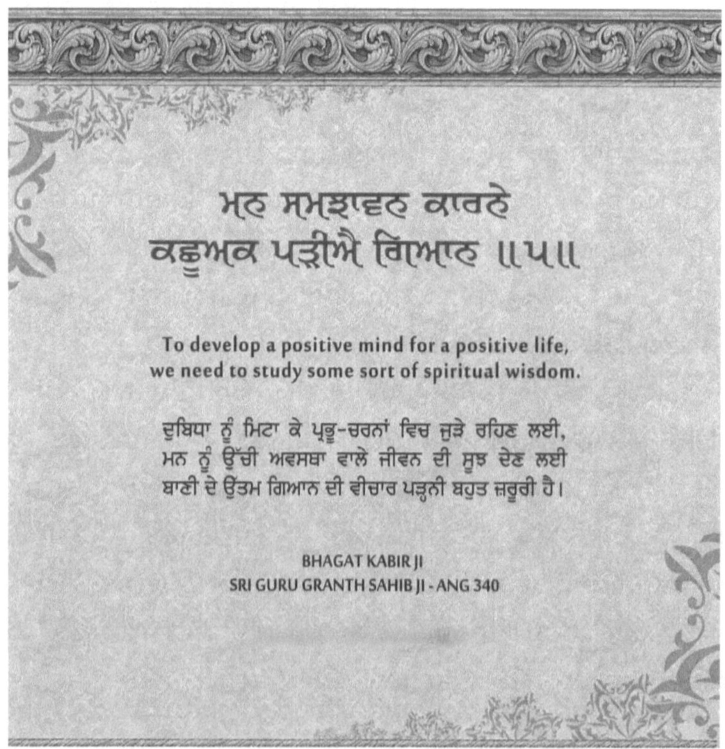

Sex

Sex refers to a physical activity between human beings that involves the genitals. Sex plays a crucial role in strengthening your emotional bond with your partner, that is why, it is strongly recommended to perform it with your life partner because if duped by your boyfriend or girlfriend, you get emotionally broken for many a decades and your life building years are wasted in haste. There's nothing wrong with desiring sex. I'm extremely sex-positive. According to the holy wisdom, sexual desire is fascinating but never ever get it fulfilled by a temporary source. Sex greed will keep on increasing and these momentary episodes of pleasure will add on dust to your body, mind and soul. Hence, there is always a right time for sex, and generally post marriage is, when the couple gets commitment, mature physically and mentally both.

The Metaphysical Approach to Sex and Marriage

The metaphysical approach portrays the marriage, as a "right to a person akin to a right to a thing, " which gives spouses "lifelong possession of each other's sexual attributes, " a transaction supposed to render sex compatible with respect for humanity.

What is more beautiful in this universe than an ecstatic big never ending kiss on your soft lips by a person whom you love with all your heart & soul. A kiss that you remember your whole life, a fulfilling kiss which fills your love tank for the years to come, a kiss where you drag each other into each other but still want more of it. A gentle still firm and promising kiss which put each and every nerve in your body on fire. A kiss which initiates a hot love affair wherein you long to merge into each other.

What is more meditative than sinking into your lover's body, feeling his/her presence deep inside you, when your breaths are in tune with the ones of your lover. Ah! the perfect state of surrender and hence eloping into the perfect moments of life which every human being on this earth must experience.

But the question here is whether you want these moments with a temporary relationship and feel miserable for the life time or you want these magnificent moments with your committed life partner and hence enjoy the marital bliss throughout life.

> *Moreover, the BIGGEST KILLERS of our body cells are fear and guilt. Beware of all the actions leading to these two emotions.*

But again, God Almighty tells us to be merged in God's name to be a bright married soul forever in life and beyond.

Holy Sri Guru Granth Sahib Ji, Ang 285

ਐਸਾ ਸੀਗਾਰੁ ਬਣਾਇ ਤੂ ਮੈਲਾ ਕਦੇ ਨ ਹੋਵਈ ਅਹਿਨਿਸਿ ਲਾਗੈ ਭਾਉ ॥

ऐसा सीगारु बणाइ तू मैला कदे न होवई अहिनिसि लागै भाउ ॥

Aisā sīgār baṇā°e ṯū mailā kaḏe na hova°ī ahinis lāgai bẖā°o.

So decorate yourself with the decorations that will never stain, and love the Lord day and night.

Pre-marital Stage

This is the 'The Golden Period' when music is in the air, bells are ringing, you have dreamy eyes, jingle in the heart, rosy dreams, romantic thoughts, flowers and gifts. This is the beauty of Courtship period.

Every new beginning is important and kindles interest and excitement. During this period a couple gets together and paves the path to a smooth, happy future. It is the time to explore, know and understand each other well. Here, it is easy to check compatibility, know the likes, dislikes, ambitions, nature and temperament of each other.

Physical attachment and attraction is a must pre-requisite between the partners before getting into such an important relationship where loving each other with devotion and honesty is of prime importance and duty. So we must assure whether we are tempted to make love to each other or not. Because love making is the most beautiful and integral part of marriage and the marriages that run without it are mostly doomed and have many sad consequences. 'And mind my pal, you only desire to make love where your emotional energy takes you to….so, endeavour purposefully to be emotionally and respectfully attached to each other'.

If in case, under the pressure of your family, peers or society, one is constrained and compromising on his / her liking for the life partner with whom one dreams of having the most blissful relationship then you actually are not justifying your role in this bond of mutual love -institution of marriage.

Always be ready to open up all your cards in front of the person you are going to marry, because if you live with secrets, you will never be able to be natural with your spouse. You will always be on tenterhooks and lead a veiled life. So be strong and have the courage to share your secret (however dark and pathetic) with your fiancée and leave it upto him to decide whether he will be able to accept and live with you for *his/her* entire life. Always remember every cloud has a silver lining and a rejection is not the end of the world. Nature is benevolent and there is abundance in this world. If the other person truly loves you, he/she will accept you with your past and can even help you to resolve your problems. And if there are any issues in current scenario it should must be given a decent burial with trust and love. But even if after meeting each other several times one doesn't develop any feelings of *likings/romance/intimacy* with *her/him* then be sure that *he/she* is not the person for you, it is not going to be an easy sail rather will be a tough call and you need to take the right decision now before its too late.

Marriage

Thus, marriage is supposed to be an unbreakable spiritual Union of two bodies, minds and souls into one. It is a mean to learn helping each other to attain together a balanced life, self-fulfillment, spiritual Unfoldment and Self-knowledge leading to perfection in life (Jeevan Pada) or purpose of life. **Marriage is the institution regulating sex, reproduction and family life.** Organization of sex and reproduction are essential to the health of the state and marriage has a special moral status and relation to the human good. Marriage (also called matrimony or wedlock) is a social union or legal contract between people called **spouses** that establishes rights and obligations between the spouses, between the spouses and their children, and between the spouses and their in-laws. The definition of marriage varies according to different cultures, but it is principally an **institution** in which interpersonal relationships, usually **intimate** and sexual, are acknowledged.

Reasons for Marriage

People marry for many reasons, including: legal, social,, emotional, financial, spiritual, and religious. Hence the principal reasons for marriage are for procreation, for complementarity, it cements relationship, it enhances interconnection between members of different families, for sexual satisfaction and on the top for companionship.

Married life, if lived with selflessness and proper understanding, will help in realizing the goal of becoming "one soul". There is no chance without the selfless attitude.

Post Marriage

- Marriage is the Union of two souls. After marriage, The Couple is the foundation of the home. Rest all is outside their boundary. Accept it or suffer for a lifetime. ਆਪੇ ਪੁਰਖੁ ਆਪੇ ਹੀ ਨਾਰੀ ॥: ***Aape purakh(u) aape hee naaree***: ਆਪੇ ਪੁਰਖੁ ਆਪੇ ਹੀ ਨਾਰੀ ॥: (sggs 1020). In the inner depth of every woman there is a man, and there is a woman in the inner depths of every man.

- ਪੁਰਖ ਮਹਿ ਨਾਰਿ ਨਾਰਿ ਮਹਿ ਪੁਰਖਾ ਬੂਝਹੁ ਬਰਹਮ ਗਿਆਨੀ ॥ ਧੁਨਿ ਮਹਿ ਧਿਆਨੁ ਧਿਆਨ ਮਹਿ ਜਾਨਿਆ ਗੁਰਮੁਖਿ ਅਕਥ ਕਹਾਨੀ ॥੩॥: Understand this, — women are born from male semen and men are born from women. The human being who connects his Awareness to God's wisdom carefully engages and adapts his life accordingly and he gets to know (see) the untold or unspoken story. ||3|| (sggs 879).

Generally, men are mostly intellectually centered and women are emotionally centered. The gap between these two centers can be narrowed or closed by balancing the complementary powers of the feminine and masculine qualities within. In nutshell, the false 'I' (**false ego-sense**) needs to vanish; for the feeling of 'I' or 'mine, mine' obstructs any possibility of inner growth and unification of Hearts. Balancing of the complementary powers and qualities, mutual respect, cooperation, and spiritual living lead to perfection in life.

LESSONS FOR WIVES here is,

Husband is your king and you are his personal secretary. He comes to your life with many negatives and many positives, relish the positives but you need to groom the negatives to make him happy, wiser and successful in your company.

LESSONS FOR HUSBANDS here is

She is your queen. Shower her all your love, give her prime importance, amend her through soft skills, listen, support and obey her small silly things. Take her side in the times of adversity, she is your life partner, both of you together have to sail through life together. None on the face of the earth is more important or essential than your soulmate or partner. Nevertheless, giving selfless respect to your parents is our prime duty.

Some key points to a peaceful romantic married life;

1. Unending and selfless respect and moral support to parents & family on both sides is solicited as this would go a long way in avoiding conflicts and clashes which tend to arise sooner or later.

2. Never ever insult your spouse in front of anyone, not even your near and dear ones like your mother, father, brother or sister. This is the biggest mistake a couple makes feeling that it was in front of my mom only, its a big taboo. Moreover if someone

tries to insult your spouse in front of you or behind you must be there to stand against it, voice your opinion and defend *him/her*. If not done, it will diminish your respect in your spouse's heart which will directly affect your love life which is the foundation of a married life along with poisoning relations with your spouse's family members.

3. It is a common scene in some cultures that a male counterpart tries to dominate a female counterpart especially in front of his mother|sister and on top of this avoids appreciating her in their presence with a perception of showing his male ego. Always remember appreciation is like a soothing balm. It irons out many wrinkles in life. In the Union of two souls there is no room for any kind of ego. Keep in mind that in case chauvinistic approach is there the relationship would never be a cherished one but just a compromise.

4. Couples should freak out together without family on regular basis to keep the spark of love alive. Love, understanding and soft open communication amongst the couple only keep them together at all levels- emotionally first- then physically- mentally- and ultimately spiritually. The foremost is emotionally. Take care of each others emotions. Please don't ridicule each other, even in person. Just nurture your togetherness.

5. Trust, the basis of any relationship must be maintained all through.

WHILE ON FAMILY WAY The child an offspring of your love in the womb is witnessing and living everything the couple lives, whether it is love|clashes|doubts|differences|trust|spirituality|harmony; so when a couple is pregnant they ought to live their life according to the kind of child they want in their arms. The infant is going to be the reflection of the life lead during the gestation period by the couple. If you have any crunch at the emotional or financial level, please don't bring one more member to feel the fire of your family. If you have a good environment in the family then please go for the child otherwise let your family be as it is and don't bring one more victim to bear the pain which your family is already bearing.

During labour pains and delivery, husband should be a part of the process, loving, encouraging and being there welcoming the baby and be the companion of the mother. To a wife, everyone else comes afterwards, first is her husband and it is watched that he is the one who is not allowed to be near to his wife during this process and elders of the home takes his place. That's really not cool. You should be both on the United front, you and your wife with no third party intervention. Both of you should be together through this journey of bringing up family. Mostly husbands leave these affairs to their moms or sisters. That's not fair. Together you are bringing a life to this earth, so together you should take care of everything. Yes, if wife is comfortable, she can take their support if lended. Every decision pertaining to the baby right from buying a diaper to the admission in a school has to be mutually decided. It's O. K. to listen the suggestions of the family members but final decision should be of the parents.

WHEN THE CHILD IS BORN

If you don't want to be a parent then you should decide it prior. But when you are already a parent, you should know how to be a parent. You should be all love to your children. You should have quality time and patience for your children. You should be a very calm, composed, firm, lively and highly understanding parent. You need to understand every stage of your growing children and act accordingly. Your role, as a parent is very crucial for the balanced mature growth of your darling child. My friend, I am coming up with all the minute intricacies and remedies on the journey of parent-child bond in my next book on 'Parenting- Being the God to your lovely child' to lend timely help to every new parent on this beautiful planet.

POST FAMILY CALL

Every couple has differences. Kindly confine them to your bedroom and sort it out in your children's absence. The simple solution here is not to react but to definitely respond at the appropriate time.

Financial planning is important part of any family. Husband & wife should together plan the family budget. If parents are staying along, they should be taken care of very well and given the pocket money they need but it is actually a couple's duty and responsibility to run the family. It brings about belongingness in both of them and keep them attached to the home. All the social obligations have to be met by them with their mutual consent on both sides of the family. If prime responsibilities of the household need to be given to the parents of the man, it should be in consensus with the perception of his wife. If imposed, it will be the major reason of family and couple conflicts.

When both of you are working as a couple it's very important to take some time out of your business schedule to be together to have romantic moments together to be with each other to meet each others' emotional, physical and spiritual needs.

PROBLEMS IN MARRIAGE

1. **Sexual dissatisfaction**: Sex is one of the drives to marriage. It draws many couples together. A couple whose relationship is built on sex is very much likely to crumble. The reason is that a spouse will only see the other one as a "sex machine". But marriage which is run without sex is also a diseased one. It is the major reason of entering into extra- marital affair. Everyone wants a whole hearted two way loving and warm communication. In many couples, they start taking each other for granted. They don't listen to each other, don't talk to each other lovingly, yell at small unaccepted stimulus, get overoccupied in work. This distorts this mersimirising bond and force the partners to look for friendship outside the bond which naturally brings a thrill missing in marriage. These platonic relationships many a times turn to physical intimacy which is a biggest threat always to the individuals and families.

> *Always remember, extra marital affair is considered as a sin as per God's words as mentioned below.*

Holy Sri Guru Granth Sahib Ji, Ang 269

ਮਿਥਿਆ ਨੇਤਰ ਪੇਖਤ ਪਰ ਤ੍ਰਿਅ ਰੁਪਾਦ ॥

मिथिआ नेत्र पेखत पर त्रिअ रूपाद ॥

Mithi▫ā netar pekhat par tari▫a rūpād.

False are the eyes which gaze upon the beauty of another's wife.

Holy Sri Guru Granth Sahib Ji, Ang 785

ਸੂਹੈ ਵੇਸਿ ਦੋਹਾਗਣੀ ਪਰ ਪਿਰੁ ਰਾਵਣ ਜਾਇ ॥

सूहै वेसि दोहागणी पर पिरु रावण जाइ ॥

Sūhai ves ḍuhāganī par pir rāvan jā‸e.

ਪਿਰੁ ਛੋਡਿਆ ਘਰਿ ਆਪਣੈ ਮੋਹੀ ਦੂਜੈ ਭਾਇ ॥

पिरु छोडिआ घरि आपणै मोही दूजै भाइ ॥

Pir chhodi‸ā ghar āpṇai mohī ḍūjai bhā‸e.

ਮਿਠਾ ਕਰਿ ਕੈ ਖਾਇਆ ਬਹੁ ਸਾਦਹੁ ਵਧਿਆ ਰੋਗੁ ॥

मिठा करि कै खाइआ बहु सादहु वधिआ रोगु ॥

Mithā kar kai khā‸i‸ā baho sāḍahu vadhi‸ā rog.

ਸੁਧੁ ਭਤਾਰੁ ਹਰਿ ਛੋਡਿਆ ਫਿਰਿ ਲਗਾ ਜਾਇ ਵਿਜੋਗੁ ॥

सुधु भतारु हरि छोडिआ फिरि लगा जाइ विजोगु ॥

Suḍh bhatār har chhodi‸ā fir lagā jā‸e vijog.

In her red robes, the discarded bride goes out, seeking enjoyment with another's husband. She leaves the husband of her own home, enticed by her love of duality. She finds it sweet, and eats it up; her excessive sensuality only makes her disease worse. She forsakes the Lord, her sublime Husband, and then later, she suffers the pain of separation from Him.

<u>Regenerate the romance in your own life partner (husband| wife) but in no way your body, mind or soul be allured towards anybody else, till the time you are in holy knot of marriage otherwise you will be exposed to many life threats which you cannot see now under the illusion of lust.</u>

So, my dear friends, it is very important to give focussed, whole hearted time to your marital bond to stay healthy, happy and sinfree throughout life.

2. **<u>Communication:</u>** For effective communication to take place the family members while sitting together must detach themselves from watching TV or flipping through newspaper or browsing on the phone, etc. This should be stopped, phones should be on vibration. Each one should listen to one another with great interest. Encouraging words should be used with one another. Avoid commenting each other when sitting together as a family and please don't speak ill of other people. It should be light, nurturing, non judgemental, growth oriented communication.

3. **<u>Improper understanding between spouses on domestic chores:</u>** Who to do what at home also constitute a problem. When one partner feels superior to the other person, there is domestic abuse and detachment. With ever changing scenarios at home front, the spouses must understand each other and volunteer need based, gender free and superiority/inferiority complex free responsibilities. Remember, my friend, Both partners complement each other.

4. **<u>Enraged family relationships:</u>** When there is lack of understanding between the couple, the couple and the family due to abc reasons, it leads to daily conflicts which in turn affects family health. It is of utmost priority to see it through magnifying glass. See, what is the underlying cause of the rage and conflicts. The couple need to make other feel that *he/she* is the most important person in his/her life. Sit together and peep into the problem openly. Discuss your emotions, feelings and underlying causes honestly. Develop mutual understanding for the smooth sail.

To give this subject thorough attention it needs, my friend, it is dealt separately in next chapter.

Chapter 6

Enraged Family Relationships

There is all bliss in living together as an understanding loving family. Living together as an understanding and supporting family should be the goal. The demons of ego and anger will definitely attack you repeatedly to destroy the peace of your family, but with God's powerful name, these demons can be won and be replaced by angelic qualities of patience, calmness, empathy and oneness.

Let's understand with the help of a story

Once a demon of conflict observed that one house had 12 members living with no conflict in their house. He wanted to see the enraged dialogues between them.

He applied magic on one of their daughter in laws while she was making the curry for the family for dinner.

She put lots of spices into that. Everybody took the dinner silently and thanked God before getting up from the dining table. When that lady took food she could not put even one spoon into her mouth. She asked everyone how come you ate it with love. Everyone hugged her and said, daily we take delicious food from your lovely hands….. how does it matters if one day it was not edible. The demon failed in his conspiracy.

He again tried another day. He, with his magic game, delayed the home returning of males of the family, who had promised their wives and children for a movie. So, they reached home one hour late from their workplace. Demon of conflict was very excited to see the enraged behaviour among the family members as he had sown the seed of annoyance.

Wonders! Males reach home, wives and children hug them and ask for their well being as they were late by one hour. They showed their concern with love, offered them water, tea and snacks. Nobody seemed annoyed because of movie being started or tickets wasted or their mood being spoiled. They were all focussed on their fathers| sons|brothers|husbands being reached home safely. Demon again failed badly. So he decided not to play any more games here in this family as they were blessed by God for having compassion, love and have already won over their respective egos and anger.

So, what we have seen is that demons will keep on attacking us till the time we are able to win the battle. And this battle can only be won by developing lots of patience and good amount of acceptance of each others' behaviour, actions, words, thoughts and most importantly;be NON-REACTIVE.

Enraged relationships - THE CAUSES AND PRACTICAL REALISTIC SOLUTIONS

Lack of understanding and non clearance of misunderstanding through constructive discussions leads to enraged relationships in the families which are a major threat to the mental & physical health of a family. In this chapter we will try to understand it from various angles. We will be insightful on the chemistry and physics of enraged relationships and will find many of its' solutions. But of course, not all the solutions, as there are many kind of family set ups and every situation has an absolutely different kind of solution. Moreover, there are always exceptions to the rules. But one thing is for sure, my friend, till the time we don't accept our real present life scenario with whole of our heart, there is going to be no peace.

Lets understand most of the root causes behind any kind of rage amongst the close relationships :

1. <u>Issue;</u>

   Different view points on various aspects of life due to which both persons/groups are not compatible for any progressive and constructive discussions.

   <u>Easy Solution;</u>

   Both parties accept it from the core of their heart that they are not made for long, healthy growth oriented discussions. They must develop peace on this front and maintain cordial relations on day to day affairs.

   Indulging in discussions and ending up in aggression leads to enraged relationship among them over the period of time.

   Yes, who knows, one fine day understanding emerges in their relationship as they have unknowingly done each other's SWOT (Strengths, Weaknesses, Opportunities and Threats).

2. <u>Issue:</u>

Attitude of both parties is opposite. One is pessimistic and other is optimistic.

<u>Easy Solution:</u>

Don't react to each other's thoughts & actions. Observe and learn if possible on various possibilities in one situation but don't comment/pull other person.

3. <u>Issue:</u>

Lifestyle and perception towards life is different. One is health conscious. Other is only money minded. One is disciplined, other is not. One indulges in gossip, other not. One is open minded other is closed.

<u>Easy Solution:</u>

Respect each other's lifestyle. You may learn from each other.

4. <u>Issue:</u>

Responsibility and authority specification. If not team players, overlapping is the major issue.

<u>Easy Solution:</u>

Sit and talk openly about the job specifications, family authority and responsibility or understand with the flow.

5. <u>Issue:</u>

Both enraged parties are operating from parent ego.

<u>Easy Solution:</u>

It must have been proven by now from your frequent conflicts that you cannot come to parent-child transactional understanding, so make efforts to reach the level of adult-adult transactions.

6. <u>Issue;</u>

One party try to control the other party.

<u>Easy solution:</u>

Let's understand, we are all controlled by Lord Almighty. And if we try to control anyone…it brings restlessness to our own soul. So, please…let other person live, my friend, …give him/her the breathing space. Nobody is puppet in anybody's hands. Earlier we understand this, the relieving it is for our own soul.

7. <u>Issue;</u>

Downgrading/Tagging/Ridiculing other person.

<u>Easy Solution:</u> God has not given anybody this right to do the above for any life in this universe. Still, if you have been doing this as an habit, abandon it right now as while abiding by this habit you will only keep on erasing all your good deeds. Appreciate others for their good qualities and show concern in person lovingly for amending the areas of improvement in other person. Remember, you may be the wisest person on earth but you should not insult or downgrade other person.

8. <u>Issue;</u>

Feeling of self sufficiency in one raged party;

Easy Solution: Please understand we are social beings. WE CANNOT LIVE WITHOUT EACH OTHER. Nobody is self sufficient. Everyone need support of each other to run the family in a smooth manner. So, every member contribute *his/her* strengths, accept others' flaws …as we are all unique.. but no body is perfect.. only God Almighty is…. and enjoy the bliss of family life.

Likewise, there are manifold issues but the easy call for any kind of issue is acceptance, empathy and open communication. These three things will develop understanding. Nevertheless, For every rage.. the outcome is pain. Try to bring peace to your own pain…think… evaluate.. brain storm…while working on this process.. you will surely end up in feeling other party's pain too. Once pain is identified, either yours or the other persons' (…cause oneness prevails…AT THE CORE, WE ARE ALL ONE)… your soul will gradually end the rage. Elevate yourself. Accept your flaws, say sorry, relieve other person of all baggages without even thinking for a second that other person is also to be blamed. To rise, to fly, my friend, you need to free yourself from the BLAME GAME.

ROLE OF A MEDIATOR:

Mediator plays a very crucial role in any of the family issues. This mediator should be unbiased and fair. Then even the issues are resolved in an amicable manner without prolonged rage.

Let's understand by taking one case study as we cannot take every household problem here. But, I promise, different Home Dynamics will be taken care in my forthcoming book.

But it is my duty to mention here that the understated situation can be vice versa also-

You can imagine DIL in place of MIL here. There are many home profiles where son is extremely attached to his mother, where DIL is extremely attached to her mother, where there can be any leaks here and there. There are thousands of scenarios-which are impossible to be covered in one chapter.

> ***But the point to be considered here is, it is of utmost importance to maintain a balance between all your close relations so that you can enjoy their beauty individually and in group dynamics.***

A Case Study   <u>Character sketch of 3 major roles in this case:</u>

MIL (Mother -In -Law) |mil- Very high ego, stubborn, rigid, perfect syndrome.

DIL (Daughter -In- law)|dil - Modern, flexible, new belief system, open minded, seek for solutions from God almighty.

SON- Obedient, dutiful, sincere and compassionate.

<u>History of the case taken</u>: Dil for 2 decades remained puppet in the control of her egoistic mil ... Conflicts were ought to happen & it was demand of the time because old is not giving space to new willingly which is law of nature and whenever you go against nature, you will have conflict and discomfort. And Some times conflicts are necessary to bring things from what they are to what they should be. Now, Dil don't want to be puppet in her hands anymore.... which was previous scene... when there were no clashes, though, cause DIL was only yes mom kind BUT she became a hub of diseases with her passive behaviour..... AND no constructive change was possible under these circumstances....

her home became a stinking place where old prevails…With no newness.

On the top, she (mil)does not want to address any discussions on the above topics because she do not want any suggestions from her dil or think out of the box. The problem here is, What she (MIL)wants is one way communication and that's it. Yes, here enraged relationships COULD HAVE BEEN PREVENTED only if DIL accepts her wisdom & mentorship whole heartedly, which is very rare scene in today's Z generation who needs to be heard and apply their genius.

<u>What does research shows: How gaps are built between mother-in-law (MIL) and daughter -in -law (DIL)</u>

1. When the son is married he has commitments to his wife and upcoming family. The emotions of son are expected in his wife too. Very true, she should respect his mother the way he does. But the scene here is that mother does not let her son respect her wife the way he loves her. Here the first gap starts between the two MIL(mother-in-law) & DIL(Daughter-in-law).

2. The new story has just begun. An educated, modern smart lady has become a new family member who wants to establish her family with her ideas and creativity but the problem arises here because mother wants to control everyone and everything in the family. So she starts giving instructions to DIL what to do what not, intervenes in new couples decisions of freaking out, having romantic time outside somewhere…here comes another gap between the two.

3. Oh!the most important place which every lady feels that I'm the boss of this place is kitchen. Husband's mother own that too and want to run it in its old fashion not allowing any new ideas to be incorporated there. Another gap.

4. Priority to attend functions from husband's relatives or wife's relatives. Now this is tug of war. Both dragging the poor boy on their side. Another gap.

> *And from here onwards, the enraged relationships begin between the two most important ladies of the house-Mother and wife. Research shows this is the major cause of conflict between husband and wife also, father in law and mother in law also, between sister in laws, between children and parents, so it need magnifying glass to peep into the problem and the solution. Many kind of scenarios are possible in the transactional analysis among relations but we are controlling here with this scenario only;*

Relationship of Married Son with his Respectful Mother

It goes without saying that every son of the world loves his mother beyond limits as she is her first lady love in this world. She is the first person to be in warm contact with and undoubetly son has stayed for nine months in her cozy womb. He has got unconditional adoration from this relation and of course, he owes a great deal to his mother. She is the one who has listened to her wholeheartedly during his important milestones and she is the one who has saved him not her from father's rage and world's harshness. When she grows old, it is his prime duty to provide her with every comfort and unconditional love of his family. This all goes pretty well till the time son is bachelor but the story changes when a new lady love comes to his life. We must understand the mother has given her whole life in nurturing her children. She deserves all the unconditional love and support now from her independent family children failing which she also has to endure a lot of pain.

Looking from All Perceptions <u>Mother-Taken here as Head of the family- Leading lady of the house</u>

She envision herself as a Dominating power to rule over the entire family... son, dil & children. Act as a Dictator. Think herself to be the wisest person of the family to run the household in her own controlled way according to her perceptions as she has given her long 40 years in building this house…absolutely true…genuine. Now, she lives in the parent ego all the time dictating her terms, planning events, decision maker in food choices, social interactions, dress choices, children career choices…wow.. true …she is so true as far as her own ego is concerned. She act as an agent to the daughters of the family as according to her they are also the basic family. She is the informant about each and every activity taking place in the family to the relatives close to her.. her daughters, sisters, brothers. CEO of the kitchen, refrigerator and the maids. Wants his son to obey him without questioniong her as done in his childhood, suppress his wife opinions and decision making power to keep on exercising her own., take decisions according to her whims and fancies whether it suits the mental frame of his wife and children or not. Expects her dil to adjust to hers' and hers' daughters nature and dictatorship without any questions and complains to her husband.

Perception of mil about her dil;

She (dil) is not receptive and not a team player. She does not adjust and is not patient. She does not know how to maintain social relationships, the way I do, does not know how to cook food the way I cook, does not know how to take care of the children. I know the proper way of doing things but my dil is totally different. She goes to work, goes to yoga classes, go to salon, wear stylish clothes…. when all this time could have been utilized in household chores. She should sit with me so that I can teach her the right methodologies of running home, obeying husband and me, being a good mother and being a good homemaker.

LESSONS FOR MILS ….

Old age is a big challenge with respect to mental, physical and emotional needs of yours. As the most respected elderly wisdom of your home, your family too needs your experience in bringing physical, mental and emotional harmony in their new brought up family. You also need your own family nearby to take care of you as you have taken good care of them your whole life. Along with that, it is the age to be enjoyed to the fullest with your positive and elevated thoughts when either your children have moved to their own lovely nests or all of you (you, your children and grand children) are fortunate enough to be living with each other. Old people are a very protective shelter to their children along with a great support system for their growing children and working ladies of the house. But alas! what do we see here in most of the joint families today is that all are living hell because of enraged relationships at homefront. As the research shows, the most enraged relationship is between mil & dil.

If at this phase of life, the elders and the married children, want to live happily with each other then here are some very important tips for everyone…but hereunder for the MIL.

1. You need to give constructive space to your dear DIL….. mentally prepare your son and daughters prior…before she comes as a newly wed bride, send her good vibes.. I'm waiting for you…I love you…this is your home…and when she comes she should practically and truthfully feel that it is her home…her ultimate destination…which she is accountable for …on the contrary what happens is…. usually mil keep on shouting and reminding, "this is my home…I am managing it from last 40 to 50 years…. you need to adjust.. you need to learn …all must and should are enforced upon her"…. remember things which are enforced may be the most beautiful and royal…gives us feeling of hell … ….

2. Just make her feel this is her home.. she is more important than your son…it is not at all difficult…if you have a right mind set up to sustain harmony and peace in your beloved son's life. Don't be possessive of your son as you were when he was a kid. He is grown up.. let the wife possess him now and you possess both of them as your most darling children…prioritise your dear dil.. and see your son will get love from his wife and you from your dil…and your

home from everyone.... your sweet young home where new abides.

3. Give importance to dil parents. Mostly, it is seen that mother being very possessive, don't let his son gel with DIL's parents….., participate where she (dil) wants you to. Don't be biased with your son to only focus on his own parents and sisters. It has to be equal both sides.

4. Give her responsibility as per her choice and consent to make her feel that she is an integral part of home…

   Benefit of the above suggestion ….. she will be occupied… mind will be busy…busy minds are better behaved…

   Give her the right and privilege to set kitchen and home as per her choice..

   Benefit….. there will be newness in the house…. she will feel strongly that it is her home…feel more belongingness towards her new home…

   Related benefit …. she will feel accountable for protecting her home from any negativity…she will do prayers…block negative contacts if any from her past life…

5. Involve her in social give and take…... rather, I would say, make her incharge of keeping all received gifts…. so that when need of giving someone something she can be asked to or discussed to bring the right gift.

6. Purchase grocery and fruits and vegetables altogether as a family…. give everyone budget…every member feel involved…and at home…even if home is being constructed or interiors done…involve children…don't hurry up… otherwise home will become a hotel…where family members are coming to sleep and enjoy their private places.

7. Have faith…. even if her behavior is not according to your expectations…. give her power through your strong positive vibes…. complaining and fighting doesn't work for good…and have faith on God almighty.. that if He has given you this challenge to bear her behaviour …don't bear this in negative sense….. to amend her behavior through soft skills …. then take it as an order from God…your own children must also had given you some challenge… she(dil) is now your own child, your prime, most cherished resposibility…yes, if you (your son and you)are not able to accept that challenge…then get separated before the onset of children…don't make them a part of hell…. We are living in abundant universe…there are many options in the world at right time.

8. Give back space to your daughters now. Let your sweet DIL now take care of them. If as an elder member of the family… you indulge in their affairs, they will never be able to develop intimacy <u>and moreover your daughters will not be able to accept new decision maker (their sister in law) in the family willingly.</u> …Moreover, …it is not possible to give your dil due respect, importance and intimacy and compassion if you already have attachment with your son and daughters. Be there, when your daughters need you, you are their mother but the point is not involving them in day to day family matters. If you are highly possessive of them…your decisions will be based on their consultancy which is going to create a conflict in your family. If any possession is needed now, its only about DIL's…. but on the contrary... what we see is…in most cases…. that….

we leave the dil for mil judgements and complaints and grudges and also making her a victim….. involving mil's daughters and sister in laws…. making her own team to put her dil down. …

9. Listen…. to children …. every member…school children… solutions to problems come by listening…. to listen more…. and speak less. Be a elevated person. Be the eldest member of the family in actuality. Bless everyone, be happy while seeing them happy. See the faults in your own born sons and daughters also and amend them with your authority. But if you see some shortcomings in your daughter in law or son in law, drift your own sons and daughters to ignore the same and encourage them to see their strengths. Being the oldest member of the family, be the most mature, impartial, keep low ego profile and accept all with widen arms.. then see how your family gives you respect and also accepts you whole heartidly as a proud head of the family who supports and advice when asked and is a strong pillar of the family.

<u>Perception of daughters of this lady</u>

Our mother deserve all the control as she has really served this household for 3 decades.

They Love giving advice asked by their mother. Loves knowing the details given by their mother as it keeps them close to their mother and their parental family. As their mother is the boss so they can put demands as per their needs. Keeps them close to their brother. Gets to know all ifs and buts of their sister in law. Can intervene easily for their neice and nephew's lives. Can rule the kitchen and home on their visits to their parental home. Wants ther sil and nephew and niece to be respectful, obedient and nice to them mother irrespective of their intervening and dominating behaviour.

LESSONS FOR the daughters of the family

1. We believe that you are darling daughters of the family but before that you are the powerful mediators for keeping your parental family on united front.

2. First lesson is not to interfere in your parental family decisions as now your sil, brother and mother, father will take all the decisions. You need to respect those decisions.

3. Develop sisterly relations with your sil. Don't gossip at her back with your mother and brother. Rather, drift both of them towards this new relation. You need to act as a catalyst in building constructive relations among all family members of your parental family.

4. Be mature and settle down happily in your own home with your husband and children. Let sil manage her own home. When you will not give shelter to your mothers' opinions (mostly unacceptable) about your sil, she will automatically start respecting her dil views.

5. When and where asked, give the most positive solutions to the family mambers.

Perception of the son

Wants everybody happy. Wants to be good son, brother, husband and a father. Desire to make a balance between all the relationships. Wants everyone to work in a team. Wants good interpersonal relations among all. Wants to gel with his new bride, wants to be her best friend, wants romantic freak outs, wants his own decision making to the food choices, school choices, career choices of his children, day to day upbringing of his kids but finds himself pissed in the presence of his mother and sisters. Wants to run the household together with his wife but at the same time his mother would not let it do, as she wants to run in her own traditional way. Feels himself sandwiched between the modern perceptions of his current family, his own and the stereotype perceptions of his mother and sister| sisters. Don't want his mother to be disrespected by his wife or children. So keep on trying to making balance between the two war fronts. So, gradually, gets tired from life. See himself grilled between values and practical life. Gets weared off from the high expectations of the honourable mother and the darling wife and loving children. Blames the institution of marriage for all this chaos and become a money making machine and a peacemaker. He starts thinking it is fault of my wife. She is not patient and she does not adjust. My mother is so good, co-operative and a good housekeeper. She cooks delicious food and is a nice lady.

LESSONS FOR SONS... in this scenario

It is the duty of the son to make a space for a new member in the family. Every lady wants to own the kitchen and run the household in her own way. Every lady wants her man to discuss social and money concerns with her first and that's absolutely the right way. If this is not acceptable to the parents and sisters of the boy, then, it is upto the family to understand that whether they want to live in daily conflicts or want a peaceful life for both- themselves and their son's. For maintaining family peace and harmony, judgements of outsiders, neighbours and relatives should not be given weightage, otherwise your family will become a hub of physical and mental diseases, as the major characters, mother and wife are not at ease.. so everyone will be dis-eased. So, take timely decision. Again, the foremost priority should be to live altogether with harmony after winning over your ego and anger, but if that awareness is not bestowed, then the arrangement as quoted beneath is the most soughted after. Again, if later in life, all members develop understanding and want to live under one roof and one kitchen, this is a going to be divine bliss. But in daily ego clashes and conflicts, you can go for one of these options which will save your family from many diseases.

1. The best call here is to live nearby but not in the same home. If financially not possible, it is always best to have two kitchens where each lady can show her skills in her own natural way. Nobody controls anyone. No conflicts. Peaceful life.

2. Husband should divide his earnings in 3 parts. His, his mother and a wife. His.. of course.. investments, his expenditure. Wife to run her kitchen, her maids and household, children expenses, her own expenditure;Mother to run her own kitchen, maids, daughters etc. Wife should know what the husband earns, mother should be contended with her share which is discussed openly as her foremost right as a darling and respected mother. This arrangement should be operated from the beginning to avoid any conflicts and before the relationships to become enraged.

Perception of the children

Wants to breathe freely in their own home. Wants their parents to give them quality time w. r. t. playing with them, their studies, helping their mom in household chores, helping them in school projects, participation in school events. Using kitchen as a laboratory to experiment new recipes. To go on family trips small and big. Expects playful atmosphere in the home. Wants harmony among every member of the family.

Perception of the daughter in law

She wants to feel at home. She want her opinions to be heard and implemented. The most important is she want her husband to listen to her and defend her when out of high expectations from dil or sil, mil or her daughters shout at her publically. She expect her husband to understand her too with same gravity as understanding her sisters and mother and involve her in important family decisions.

LESSONS FOR DILS.. in this scenario

1. This world is a garden of different flowers, accept the colours and the fragrance as it is, because you neither have power nor you have any control or any judging authority to change them from their originality, just go away from the poisonous plants or flowers, befriend with the fragrant ones, abide in good company-those who are near to God, talk about God, bring you near to Him. And remember-Work is worship…. engross yourself in your work deeply.. Be very busy.

2. Its very important to make positive affirmations to start the day in a dynamic manner. And even it is more important to believe in your own self.. :)LOVE YOURSELF so that you are able to perculate this love in the family.

3. Knowing others is wise, knowing yourself is enlightenment. You are strong, worthy, valuable and necessary. These affirmations should be integral part of your lifestyle. You consider yourself as light in the darkness. Be joyful, Say yes to life, have fun and project positivity all around you. This attitude will make you like a sun in the centre and people wanting to be near you. Live your life in a wholesome way reciting God's name, pursuing your hobbies, doing your assigned duties in a family and live free, happy and young forever. You are the core of your family. When you become a catalyst of contagious happiness, your family will also reflect joy in a holistic manner.

<u>Here a story of carrot, coffee and eggs is very important to share.</u>

Once a daughter was not able to adjust in her in laws. She cried and called her mother to take her back. Mother being very wise, called her to stay with her for a week's time. She took her to her favourite restaurants, to her favourite wardrobe outlets for first three days. Then on fourth day, she took her to the kitchen. She asked her to keep three pans filled with water on the flames. In first pan she put eggs, in second carrots and in third coffee beans. After being boiled for 20 minutes, mother asked her daughter to remove the lids one by one from all three pans.

On removing lid from pan of eggs, she explained this is first kind of persons who become hostile (as the eggs have become hard inside)after passing through harsh realities of life|adjusting with different personalities|coping with change. They are irritated, frustrated and angry most of the times, so not living at peace. On removing lid of the carrots' pan, mother explained these are second category of persons who become highly passive, pitiable, dependent on others' opinions and decisions. They lose their unique nature and magnificient originality like carrots have, after facing the 20 minutes stay in boiling water. Mother then ask her daughter this question, would you like to be like eggs or carrots? The daughter replied, mama, you know me so well. Neither I want to be hostile nor I want to be pitiable. I am a educated smart girl. Please show me the better way to meet the change. Then they open third lid of coffee beans. The moment it is opened there is aroma of coffee in the air and coffee has changed the very colour of adversity to its own colour. Then mother explained, this is third kind of persons, who are able to change the very nature and behaviour of adversity with their soft and life skills. Now, tell me, would you like to be like coffee beans. She immediately nodded yes and asked for the guidance to become the same.

Mother gave following tips,

➢ Listen whole heartedly to every member of the family.

➢ Don't judge other person, he /she must have his/her reasons for behaving the way he/she is behaving.

> Don't react. Wait for other person to be calm to discuss the matter where you should give your point of view and show your concern in amicable manner.

> Accept other person the way he/she is. Don't ever analyse.

> When you are right, take stand. Where needed critically, you can take our support|discuss with me or dad.

> Keep yourself busy in constructive tasks of self and family care.

> Don't ever tell every activity of your home to me. Enjoy your family in your own way and simultaneously solve your day to day problems yourself.

Daughter went home and lived happily thereafter with her husband, children, mother in law, father in law and sister in laws. Now, DIL listening to her soul voice, break her ego barriers but is not a puppet in anybody's hands…. which was previous scene…

4. Be invisible leader for your family….. take responsibility to make it heaven …by avoiding confrontations…. not entrying into power games of others…. …let them enjoy their power…you enjoy peace and bliss by doing and giving the family what they want…and listening to each one of them…meeting their needs…channelizing their negative energies into positive by proactive actions…. involving other universal forces by theory of oneness and cause and effect. (…if we do good to any souls…souls which are in our preview will definitely get the light and benefit).

5. Strengthen your faith …. recite on God's name again and again.. listen…speak …. recitation in silence… …pray, discuss, cry, share… with God….. He will immediately send one or more of His saviours to rescue you.. free you

130

from your pain and give you solution in way or other.... He is capable beyond any limit, time and space..... He can change the sofwares and intentions of His beings in Favour of your true intentions.

6. Try to see His light in every soul. If any soul gives you challenge-it is His order...accept it deligently...and smilingly...it's the trial for your strength and applying it in practicality...so understand this mystery in simple way... if somebody yelling at you...aggressive with you .... complaining you.... be still.. listen it whole heartidily... as complaint is a gift.... its' a kind of your patience test.... puzzle given to you to solve...God is teaching you to win over your ego..... ...for which there is no medicine other than God's name.... so understand that God has been so merciful to you in helping you to win over that big force.... it will be difficult for you to implement this in the beginning but will be easy to thrive in this negative world as a smooth sail .... rest of your life...so say "God help me" if you have to deal with high egos of any characters around you...as .... these characters are also operating under order of God.

Holy Sri Guru Granth Sahib Ji, Ang 291

ਆਪਨ ਖੇਲੁ ਆਪਿ ਵਰਤੀਜਾ ॥

आपन खेलु आपि वरतीजा ॥

Āpan khel āp vartījā.

ਨਾਨਕ ਕਰਨੈਹਾਰੁ ਨ ਦੂਜਾ ॥੧॥

नानक करनैहारु न दूजा ॥१॥

Nānak karnaihār na dujā. ||1||

He Himself has staged His own drama;O Nanak, there is no other Creator. ||1|

The Conclusion:

The above thumbrules if followed diligently will definitely lead to a divine bliss in your own respective homes|lives…but alas not everywhere and seldom these lessons are practically adhered by the families.. so rage in the family begins which gradually leads to enraged relationships. As the time goes on, the taste of relation increase, either it becomes more sweet or more salty and that depends upon on what you daily adds to it.

> *And at last, my friend, I would like to mention that 'One who knows how to live, will live happy without any comforts. Those who don't know how to live will be found sad and gloomy inspite of all the comforts. Life is not a music player where YOU can listen to your favourite songs. It is a radio in which whatever is being played be happy with that.*

Rigidity in behavior and belief system is the root cause of failure and bitterness in relationships….. as man is a social animal, relationships are of utmost importance in life …. as the worst punishment given to any hardcore criminal is isolation.

Patience and politeness are not our weaknesses, they are infact the reflection of our inner strength…. never lose them in life. Take the protection and guideline of Truthful, positive and pure God's name for keeping you protected from the demons of anger and ego to enjoy harmonious family bliss.

We can avoid these rages by individually working on our weaknesses. Because if we want to enjoy each others' company in a beautiful big family, we need to be patient and win over our respective ego. But the foremost is the married couple. If wife and husband fail to become 'one', the consequences could lead to a devastating instability of the entire family — divorce, separation, broken family, arguments, litigation, violence, depression, suicide and even murders. On account of the foolishness and selfishness of adults, children suffer the most. When we look upon the other person as part of us, all the differences disappear. This is the High Road, of course many are unwilling to take.

- ਸਰਬ ਭੂਤ ਏਕੈ ਕਰਿ ਜਾਨਿਆ ਚੂਕੇ ਬਾਦ ਬਿਬਾਦਾ ॥: *Sarab bhoot ekai kari jaaniaa chookae baad bibaadaa*: I look upon all beings alike, and my conflict and strife are ended (sggs 483).

Differences or lack of oneness rise on account of the negative tendencies such as lust, anger, greed, attachment, pride and their numerous variations like selfishness (the feeling of 'mine, mine'), enviousness, stubborn mindedness, judgmental behavior, etc., which leads to resentment, conflicts, tension and disharmony. In the selfish world, generally love lasts so long one is healthy and keeps bringing in the paycheck (i. e., income). For some reason (e.g., illness, misfortune, etc.), the day the paycheck stops, love also disappear as horns from the head of a donkey!

> ***Sometimes, one person also act as a strong catalyst in saving peace and unity in the family but that one person need to have a high level of awareness on human relations and dwell as an enlightened soul. To attain this level, its very importort to abide by God's words and follow it judiciously. God's name is the only powerful tool to win over powerful demons of lust, attachment, greed, anger and ego. And once, these vices are won, there is no point of conflict with this person and he/she will act as a role model for other family members.***

<u>Strive to be this kind of person and save your family from the enraged relationships because happiness is family.</u>

<u>FLOATERS, FIGHTERS AND NAVIGATORS</u>

Life is like being in a boat going down a river. Some stretches of the river are smooth and quiet; other parts are turbulent and filled with rapids. People react in one of three ways.

Some people are floaters. They passively resign themselves to accept the river in its present condition. They aimlessly go along for the ride.

Others are fighters. They try to fight the forces of nature at every point, but eventually experience burnout, stress, depression, irritation or addiction.

A third group are navigators. They realize they can't control the river. They can, however, equip themselves to navigate the river. Navigators learn to read the river and respond to it appropriately. They "know the flow" and then they "go with the flow. "

The excerpt above is a summary of a section in Kevin McCarthy's book entitled The On-Purpose Person. Let's consider the ramifications of that categorization of people.

Would you characterize yourself as a floater or a fighter? In other words, do you passively resign yourself to the circumstances of your life and just go along for the ride? Or do you find yourself in adversarial relationships with everyone and everything around you? The first response will rob you of any control in your life. The second response will rob you of any comfort in your life.

Consider the third alternative, that of navigator. A navigator does not naively think he is in control of all aspects of his life. He realizes there are some givens in life he has to accept. On the other hand, he is not overwhelmed with the assumption he has no control on any of the aspects of his life.

Look at your life. What are some of the givens you have to accept? What are some variables over which you have control? What are some things you know you will be facing in the days ahead? How can you prepare for them? Floaters aimlessly go along for the ride. Fighters strike out at everything and everybody in random anger. Navigators "know the flow" and then they "go with the flow. "

Transpose yourself now into the life of the church. Are you a floater in the life of the church, someone who passively resigns himself to what's going on with the assumption, "A handful of people are going to make the decisions anyway, so what say do I have in the matter?"

Or are you a fighter? Do you put yourself in an adversarial relationship with those around you, always suspicious that someone is trying to put something over on you?

Let me suggest the third alternative as a better way. Be a navigator in the life of the church. This means to:

- Accept some givens in the life of the church over which you have no control.

- Investigate your own life to see what competencies and gifts you bring to the table.

- Dream about what you want the church to be.

- Look for ways in which you can have input into the ministries of the church.

- Pray for God's guidance for all who are in positions of leadership.

- Sense where you think God is at work.

- Based on your intelligent and prayer-saturated perspective, jump in with both feet with calm and composed mind.

- Learn to manage your anger if it knocks at your door.

Chapter 7

Anger Management

'Anger is One Word Short of Danger'

Why do we get angry? What are its consequences on us and our loved ones? What is anger at the first place. Anger is a strong reaction towards unacceptable stimulus from the environment. It is so strong that in few seconds an angry person can put his or the victim's life at stake. It is such a powerful emotion that it forces you to react immediately to the person who has made you angry.

We can relate so many examples from the surroundings where brother kills his brother, father is brutal to his son, husband is violent to his wife. In the movie "Thapad" we see the consequences of slapping a loved wife in public in a famiy get together. Although she being a pregnant woman, they're divorced on the genuine plea of weak relationship where wife is given a slap on a trivial matter. Jails are filled with persons who committed various crimes under the influence of anger.

<u>**So, let's not underestimate the anger. Anger is very powerful emotion which needs to be kept under control for so many realistic reasons;**</u>

1. To save relations where we really love them, our wife, husband, children, parents, brothers and sisters.
2. To save our goodwill in our surrounding in front of our family, neighbours, friends and colleagues.

137

3. To maintain our peace of mind. We are not able to create anything productive under the rage of anger.

4. To enjoy harmony in our home sweet home. Anger being contagious spreads from one member of the family to another. Just imagine husband yells and shouts on his wife in the morning before leaving home for the office. It is transmitted to the children in no time, then it is transmitted to the elders in the family or from elders to the wife/children then to the maids. Then maids carry it in their home. Pandemic of anger spreads with one burst of anger behaviour. Many minds get polluted and homes get destroyed with the same. So, to maintain harmony in the home front, it is very important to learn how to control anger.

5. To survive the productive office, 'Angry boss' doesn't make a productive office. Employees waste much of their time in thinking why were they being shouted. Finding themselves helpless and in need of money, they keep on cursing and working. The entire atmosphere of office is spoiled. Similar is the scenario at home front also, in stress, children, spouse and elders are not able to live the life they are meant to live.

<u>Why do we get angry?</u>

There are 3 prime reasons for the same.

1. We expect a lot from other person.
2. My perception is different from other person.
3. I want other person to be like me.

Anger is one word less than D- ANGER. Many mental health problems are caused in persons of any age and gender because of becoming the victim of anger of someone close in their surroundings. I have come across many cases of wife/child being mentally ill because of angry nature of the spouse/father respectively.

1. Case of Yuvraj Singh (age 21 years)

    (Victim of anger of parents – self esteem got low)

2. Case of Catherine (Age 45 years)

    (Victim of husband's anger bursts in the morning -her productivity and peace were affected)

3. Case of Angelina (8 years)

A banker reached home with the office chaos and environment in his mind. He had to take an international interview at 10:00p.m. He took tea with his mother and then looked for his mobile phone. He found it drenched in the glass of water. He was very furious. He found his 8 year old daughter in the room. Without waiting to know how mobile went into the glass, he gave four tight slaps to her little darling daughter. She got so scared that she started and kept crying for around 2 hours. Under the influence of fear and hatred for his father she got very high fever. She got 100 and 4 fever, immediately ambulance was called and she was shifted to hospital because she was not even able to breathe. She was kept in hospital for 4 days. When she was asked in the hospital about the phone, she told it was her younger brother who was 2 years old who put it in the glass of water. By the time, she noticed, it was already drenched and before she could tell her father, she got the slaps. So, father in the rage of anger and the reactive mode did really wrong by giving slaps to the innocent person.

<u>Story of son & mother</u>

(Son hanged to death in his youth because he killed his friend in rage. He was not reprimanded & counseled timely for loose temper in the childhood)

<u>Story of father and son</u>

To save his son from losing his temper at small stimulus, father asked his son to fit nails on the fence around their small cute garden. Son did so. After few days, he asked to remove them. He was agitated first that why at the first place his dad got them fixed but then he obeyed his father and removed the nails. Father went to the venue with his darling son and showed him the unremovable marks of the removed nails on the beautiful fence. Then he explained, this is how our anger bursts leave unremovable scars on our beautiful relations which gets removed after many decades. So, don't lose temper at small stimulus. Be calm when things don't go your way. Wait. When the air is clear from angry vibes, discuss the issue and find the solution. There is a key to every lock, so there are solutions to every problem. But problems get aggravated with rage. And problems get solution with discussions.

To conclude it is always preferred to maintain your clam and offer appropriate solutions to the person who get angry. When somebody shouts/yells use wrong body language /gestures /verbal abuse to you. . . . . you always have two options;

1. To revert back & then automatically give rise to hot argumentation or blasting conflicts.
2. To remain calm and composed/ respond to situation to the person who got angry at appropriate time.

But if you choose first option & show your grudges/anger, it may explode and you or other person may get nervous breakdown, some crimes may happen or you will end the relationship or you will convert the relationship into bitter one. Remember, whatever you speak when you are angry. . . . . will be reflected in your mind again & again and give you mental agony. So, solution is, let the people live with their perception (right or wrong) and you live in your own perception.

Don't try to change anyone, it is impossible. If people are enemies of your life style & happiness. Let go, ignore. Detach yourself emotionally (not physically or worldly or mentally) from the very relation, due to which you get bitter or salty memories or regrets related to the person. Don't bother. Keep yourself fit & healthy in all conditions. Both parties in conflict are right in their own way. Don't keep ill feeling for anyone. . they have their own back-ups to be like that. You, in which the God abides, is your only truefriend or your own worst enemy.

<u>REMEDIES TO KEEP ANGER IN CONTROL</u>

ਆਪਣ ਹਥੀ ਆਪਣਾ ਆਪੇ ਹੀ ਕਾਜੁ ਸਵਾਰੀਐ ॥੨੦॥

Aapan Hathhee Aapanaa Aapae Hee Kaaj Savaareeai ||20||

With our own hands, let us resolve our own affairs. ||20||

ਆਸਾ ਵਾਰ (ਮਃ ੧) (੨੦):੫ - ਗੁਰੂ ਗਰੰਥ ਸਾਹਿਬ : ਅੰਗ ੪੭੪ ਪੰ. ੩

Raag Asa Guru Nanak Dev

1. FIRST VERY simple but most important remedy is to be absolutely non-reactive and completely silent at the time of (the moment of) strong annoying reaction or words or actions or gestures from anyone. It will save you from the blast. When you are non- reactive to other's disturbing languages (verbal/non-verbal) you immediately save yourself from the storm of your anger emotions. Remember - Reactions are always immature but responses are always mature/wise and solution oriented.

2. Second step, after doing first remedial task of being silent, start counting some holy mantra (that you remember from the heart) if not applicable, start counting from 20 to 1 immediately and I promise, incorporating these first two remedies will wave off your anger for the particular situation.

3. Then, the third action on your part should be to leave that place/person for a peaceful environment. Otherwise that annoying stimulus will again prompt you to react. The best is make an excuse with a smile and go/leave to your room/ toilet/common room etc.

4. Then to calm yourself do counting meditation for a minute. Counting your breaths on finger count 15 times in one go, Doing it 4 times i. e. 15*4 = 60sec = 1 min. This 1 minute meditation will make you calm and composed.

5. Now, that you are clam, you can give thought to what happened and think rationally. Don't take it personally and get annoyed again. See, the other person is suffering from some psychological disorder, inferiority complex, superiority complex, fear, guilt, or insecurity or attachment.

6. Bless the other person. If your situation demands clearing of the air, go to other person and talk in an assertive manner. Respond with solution in hand. You should be clear what you will tolerate and what not. Express it clearly and with confidence.

- **<u>If anger is frequent,</u>**

1. Make a journal, register how many times you get anger bursts in a day.
2. Find out the root cause of your anger
3. Keep away from the stimulus that trigger your anger
4. Do daily practices of Meditation/ Exercise / Prayers for staying in Gratitude mode.
5. Label yourself and others positively. Words have power.

Words have power either negative or positive. .... we keep on recalling ...oh! he|she said me those words.... . why?. . . . . We remember the negative words and they keep on striking in the mind again and again making a thought pattern. One small negative thought when repeatedly thought will bring dangerous consequences of hatred, broken relationships, broken homes, mental disorders or even crime. Only when we attach ourselves to God's name that we are liberated from these negative thoughts. When we are daily reading positivity, positive words initiate positive thoughts which in turn brings on forefront loving, warm, calm and composed nature.

- Understand Souls and Karmic Connections. We have through many lifetimes lived with many different souls in the form of family, friends or enraged relations (those who don't really get along with us). Some may have even tried to harm us emotionally, physically or spiritually. All vice versa. All said and done, we are all the same and belong to only one group that is SOULS. We all have travelled together in different lifetimes and have shared various relationships with each other. Each person is a soul that tries to help the other move forward spiritually and reduce the Karmic baggage. Sometimes the soul that loves us the most, might willingly take birth as an enemy or a tormentor in a lifetime, just to help us work out our karma. Thus, a person, whom we think hates us and we in return hate him/her, might be our greatest well-wisher spiritually. He or She may be given the responsibility for we being transformed to becoming spiritual or compassionate. That very person who is creating hell in our lives may bring us closer to spirituality or he/she may be doing so because that could be the only way to teach us a lesson. Sometimes, a soul is reborn just to comfort us and be there in times of need.

So, who is our friend and who is our enemy? They are all part of the Soul- Family who want to help us and want help in return. Sometimes an opportunity comes in the form of a disaster. Sometimes, the only way to grow spiritually and in life is through pain, sorrow and turmoil. That is when Life seems strange. Hence never form judgements, abuse or hate and never say nasty things about anyone. Who knows we may be harming the soul who loves us the most spiritually but are not able to recognize it as the soul is wearing a different body mask in this particular lifetime.

> ***So resolve your issues with everyone. I know, You have been so hard on yourself. Now, ... Take a moment. . . . , Sit back. . . . , Reflect at your Life.***
>
> ***Reflect -at the grief that softened you,*** **at the heartache that strengthened you.**

<u>Despite everything, you are still growing- so, my dear friend, Be proud of this.</u>

"Start a new trend. Stop saying 'sorry'instead say 'Thanks'. For instance, in place of 'Sorry I am late' say ' Thank you for waiting for me'. This will shift the way you think for yourself and improve your relationships with others who get to receive your 'Gratitude' instead of 'Negativity'."

➤ Operating from Spiritual Mode/not in human mode

- Everything Happens For A Reason. Nothing Occurs By Chance. Let your Life Reflect The Faith You Have In God. Fear Nothing And Pray About Everything.

- Be Strong, Trust God's Word, Trust The Process And Go Where He Leads You. It's All Part Of God' s Divine Plan! You only strive to become Love, Smile, Encouragement and full of Life. That's the real You. Start your journey towards real you today. Don't focus on repairing the old but concentrate on building the new. The persons who envy, jealous, gossip, criticize you with annoyed face (when you look at them / or talk to them you get such vibes as if world is a dull/ dead/ or annoying place) but please don't bother about that. 'Cause this is contrary. This magnificient world is a beautiful and wonderful place to live in. It is because they carry such negative aura (maybe for you. . . if they' re different for others) but don't let their negative energy affect you and steal your beautiful smile & enthusiasm. Fake giving smile till you naturally start giving it, inspite of negative aura of a person with whom you are closely associated either in home or office. When the other person is not the same as you expect, you operate from the spiritual mode and understand that the other person is in the human mode.

You add highest value to the person/situation infront of you irrespective of the ego, insecurity, fear, greed, inferiority or superiority levels of the next person.

You just do your karma. You are able to give love, compassion, communicate freely to the other person & understand his/her pain. Means you empathise with the difficulties other person is passing through, which may be the cause of his/her uneasiness/ discomfort or irritation. When you lead by compassion and not by the prejeduice, you set example for your children to behave the same way when they come in such a situation. So, indirectly you are leading and showing how to communicate and resolve the conflicts in difficult situations & difficult people. Some times conflicts are necessary to bring things from what they are to what they should be but remember resolving them at the right time is of utmost importance.

Chapter 8

Befriending God

If you realize that God stands beside you, when others cast stones, you will never be afraid, never feel worthless and never feel alone. God is always there. He's there when a friend disappoints you. He's there when it's cold, lonely and sad. He's there, no matter what your story of life is. Put everything in God's hands and all the worries will go away. We spend our whole life seeking the glory of God but my friend, remember, He is omnipresent and everready to lend His helping hand.

Holy Sri Guru Granth Sahib Ji, Ang 784

ਹਉ ਸੰਮਲਿ ਥਕੀ ਜੀ ਓਹੁ ਕਦੇ ਨ ਬੋਲੈ ਕਉਰਾ ॥

हउ समलि थकी जी ओहु कदे न बोलै कउरा ॥

 Haⁿo sammal thakī jī oh kaḏe na bolai kaⁿurā.

ਕਉੜਾ ਬੋਲਿ ਨ ਜਾਨੈ ਪੂਰਨ ਭਗਵਾਨੈ ਅਉਗਣੁ ਕੋ ਨ ਚਿਤਾਰੇ ॥

कउड़ा बोलि न जानै पूरन भगवानै अउगणु को न चितारे ॥

Kaⁿuṛā bol na jānai pūran bhagvānai aⁿugaṇ ko na chiṯāre.

ਪਤਿਤ ਪਾਵਨੁ ਹਰਿ ਬਿਰਦੁ ਸਦਾਏ ਇਕੁ ਤਿਲੁ ਨਹੀ ਭੰਨੈ ਘਾਲੇ ॥

पतित पावनु हरि बिरदु सदाए इकु तिलु नही भंनै घाले ॥

Paṯiṯ pāvan har biraḏ saḏāⁿe ik ṯil nahī bhannai ghāle.

ਘਟ ਘਟ ਵਾਸੀ ਸਰਬ ਨਿਵਾਸੀ ਨੇਰੈ ਹੀ ਤੇ ਨੇਰਾ ॥

घट घट वासी सरब निवासी नैरै ही ते नेरा ॥

Ghaṯ ghaṯ vāsī sarab nivāsī nerai hī ṯe nerā.

ਨਾਨਕ ਦਾਸੁ ਸਦਾ ਸਰਣਾਗਤਿ ਹਰਿ ਅੰਮ੍ਰਿਤ ਸਜਣੁ ਮੇਰਾ ॥੧॥

नानक दासु सदा सरणागति हरि अम्रित सजणु मेरा ॥१॥

Nānak ḏās saḏā sarṇāgaṯ har amriṯ sajaṇ merā. ||1||

I have grown weary of testing Him, but still, He never speaks harshly to me. He does not know any bitter words; the Perfect Lord God does not even consider my faults and demerits. It is the Lord's natural way to purify sinners; He does not overlook even an iota of service. He dwells in each and every heart, pervading everywhere; He is the nearest of the near. Slave Nanak seeks His Sanctuary forever; the Lord is my Ambrosial Friend.

There are two kinds of people; those who say to God, ' dear God, everything is yours, please see how to abandon my worries. I trust you. I know you love me and I love you too. ' and those who say to God 'I am so worried and I will do it my way. '

There is a popular story related to this, "a poor man fixed his daughter's marriage in a well to do family and now is worried about how he is going to spend so much money on her marriage as expected by her in laws. He kept on stressing himself until frustrated as to how he is going to do all this saying himself again and again, "how will I marry my daughter". emphasis was 'on my daughter' again and again, alas! No hope was coming his way. One day, in the deep worry & helplessness, he prayed humbly to God that "please help, please take care of your daughter, she is your daughter and you need to device a path to marry her", he prayed wholeheartidly to God, and dear God in no time answered by throwing a 'situation' in his life. This poor labourer saw a child drowning in front of him when he was working in the fields near the river. Being a helpful human being, without wasting any time, he jumped into the river and saved the child. In no time a very rich merchant appeared who thanked him for saving his son's life. His son was playing near the river while he was busy hunting in the forest near that village. He prized him with lots of money and bounties as a return gift for his boy's life. With this money, the poor man married his daughter gracefully and she lived happy thereafter. So, see God lend us immediate help by sending his persons wherever we are. He is the commander of the whole universe. We have a very small area of control, but God has the entire universe under his control. So, never ever keep the worries in your hands and think of solutions beyond your control. Surrender. Pray. Keep God on your side. Efforts, of course are needed, because God help those who help themselves.

Holy Sri Guru Granth Sahib Ji, Ang 778

ਜਿਸੁ ਸਿਮਰਤ ਦੁਖੁ ਕੋਈ ਨ ਲਾਗੈ ਭਉਜਲੁ ਪਾਰਿ ਉਤਾਰਾ ॥

जिसु सिमरत दुखु कोई न लागै भउजलु पारि उतारा ॥

Jis simrat ḍukh koꞌī na lāgai bha°ojal pār uṭārā.

Remembering Him in meditation, pain does not touch me; thus I cross over the terrifying world-ocean.

He is on our side when we are pure and positive inside.

When we are dwelled in right thinking. Now witness signs of right/ wrong thinking

Right thinking

Be confident that you are right when you think on below lines;

- Constructive relationships
- Winning on your ego
- Interdependence
- Letting go and accepting people and situations as they are
- Service to all

Wrong thinking

Be SURE that you are WRONG when you think on below lines;

- Destructive relations
- Independent behaviour

- Segregating family members
- Operating from Ego
- Authority feelings

When you are on wrong track of thoughts even meditation is not possible.

When we can participate in the sorrow as well as happiness of others, when we are ready to serve his people with all our capability and skills, God always keep us in his blessed zone as a gesture of his parental love for us. And when God decides to bless you, He will cause situations to come in our favour.

1. Believe in only Supreme Power-Befriend only Almighty

ਜਾ ਕਾ ਮੀਤੁ ਸਾਜਨੁ ਹੈ ਸਮੀਆ ॥

Jaa kaa meethsaajan hai sameeaa ||

Those who have the lord as their friend and companion

ਤਿਸੁ ਜਨ ਕਉ ਕਹੁ ਕਾ ਕੀ ਕਮੀਆ ॥੧॥

This jan ko kahu kaa kee kameeaa ||1||

– tell me, what else do they need? ||1||

2. He heals, He befriends you, He forgives you, He accepts you, He loves you, He listens to you, He makes you kind, He makes you powerful, He makes you lovely, He makes you Divine Bliss.

ਹਰਿ ਕਾ ਨਾਮੁ ਜਪਤ ਦੁਖੁ ਜਾਇ ॥

Har kaa naam japathdhukhjaae ||

Chanting the name of the lord, sorrow is dispelled.

ਨਾਨਕ ਬੋਲੈ ਸਹਜਿ ਸੁਭਾਇ ॥੪॥

Naanakbolaisehajsubhaae ||4||

O nanak, chant it with intuitive ease. ||4||

3. God is waiting for us to hug us and give us abundant joy.

> *Remember, my dear friend;*
> *As a parent has utmost love for his\her child, so is the*
> *love of dear God for us. He only wants us to be safe,*
> *happy and truthful.*

Always keep God on your side

ਜਾ ਤੂ ਮੇਰੈ ਵਲਿ ਹੈ ਤਾ ਕਿਆ ਮੁਹਛੰਦਾ ॥

Ja thoo maerai val hai tha kia muhashhandha ||

When you are on my side, lord, what do I need to worry about?

ਅੰਮ੍ਰਿਤ ਕੀਰਤਨ ਗੁਟਕਾ: ਪੰਨਾ ੧੬੨ ਪੰ. ੧੩

raag maaroo guru arjan dev

ਤੁਧੁ ਸਭੁ ਕਿਛੁ ਮੈਨੋ ਸਉਪਿਆ ਜਾ ਤੇਰਾ ਬੰਦਾ ॥

Thudhh sabh kishh maino soupia ja thaera bandha ||

You entrusted everything to me, when I became your slave.

ਅੰਮ੍ਰਿਤ ਕੀਰਤਨ ਗੁਟਕਾ: ਪੰਨਾ ੧੬੨ ਪੰ. ੧੪

raag maaroo guru arjan dev

ਲਖਮੀ ਤੋਟਿ ਨ ਆਵਈ ਖਾਇ ਖਰਚਿ ਰਹੰਦਾ ॥

Lakhamee thott n avee khae kharach rehandha ||

My wealth is inexhaustible, no matter how much I spend and consume.

ਅਮ੍ਰਿਤ ਕੀਰਤਨ ਗੁਟਕਾ: ਪੰਨਾ ੧੬੨ ਪੰ. ੧੫

raag maaroo guru arjan dev

ਲਖ ਚਉਰਾਸੀਹ ਮੇਦਨੀ ਸਭ ਸੇਵ ਕਰੰਦਾ ॥

Lakh chouraseeh maedhanee sabh saev karandha ||

The 8. 4 million species of beings all work to serve me.

ਅਮ੍ਰਿਤ ਕੀਰਤਨ ਗੁਟਕਾ: ਪੰਨਾ ੧੬੨ ਪੰ. ੧੬

raag maaroo guru arjan dev

ਏਹ ਵੈਰੀ ਮਿਤਰੁ ਸਭਿ ਕੀਤਿਆ ਨਹ ਮੰਗਹਿ ਮੰਦਾ ॥

Eaeh vairee mithr sabh keethia neh mangehi mandha ||

All these enemies have become my friends, and no one wishes me ill.

ਅਮ੍ਰਿਤ ਕੀਰਤਨ ਗੁਟਕਾ: ਪੰਨਾ ੧੬੨ ਪੰ. ੧੭

raag maaroo guru arjan dev

ਲੇਖਾ ਕੋਇ ਨ ਪੁਛਈ ਜਾ ਹਰਿ ਬਖਸੰਦਾ ॥

Laekha koe n pushhee ja har bakhasandha ||

No one calls me to account, since God is my forgiver.

ਅਮ੍ਰਿਤ ਕੀਰਤਨ ਗੁਟਕਾ: ਪੰਨਾ ੧੬੨ ਪੰ. ੧੮

raag maaroo guru arjan dev

ਅਨੰਦੁ ਭਇਆ ਸੁਖੁ ਪਾਇਆ ਮਿਲਿ ਗੁਰ ਗੋਵਿੰਦਾ ॥

Anandh bhaeia sukh paeia mil gur govindha ||

I have become blissful, and I have found peace, meeting with the guru, the lord of the universe.

ਅੰਮ੍ਰਿਤ ਕੀਰਤਨ ਗੁਟਕਾ: ਪੰਨਾ ੧੬੨ ਪੰ. ੧੯

raag maaroo guru arjan dev

ਸਭੇ ਕਾਜ ਸਵਾਰਿਐ ਜਾ ਤੁਧੁ ਭਾਵੰਦਾ ॥੭॥

Sabhae kaj savariai ja thudhh bhavandha ||7||

All my affairs have been resolved, since you are pleased with me. ||7||

ਅੰਮ੍ਰਿਤ ਕੀਰਤਨ ਗੁਟਕਾ: ਪੰਨਾ ੧੬੨ ਪੰ. ੨੦

raag maaroo guru arjan dev

4. **To make the most of your time, take time to pray. Pray as if everything depends on God.**

We are divine enough to ask and we are important enough to receive.

> *"Pray trust, receive in abundance, don't limit yourself in stress when you are right and true. . . . . . ."* **Remember only him. Talk only to Him.**

ਸਰਬ ਰੋਗ ਕਾ ਅਉਖਦੁ ਨਾਮੁ ॥

Sarab rog kaa aoukhadh naam ||

The naam is the panacea, the remedy to cure all ills.

5. When we meditate on God, He takes away all our botherations

Moreover, He fills us with positivity, hope and faith and all tasks get done beautifully- automatically, so that you can smile all the time and spread it all around you. And smile is cooling system of heart, sparkling system of eyes, lighting system of brain and releasing system of mind. So, activate all systems with your sweet smile.

6. God is the best listener - you don't need to shout, nor cry out loud. Because He hears even the very silent prayer of a sincere heart.

When you turn your worry into worship, God will turn your battles into blessings.

7. Meditation minimize our thoughts

We all get multiple thoughts in a day and during night according to the information stored in our subconscious mind. It is important to slow down the speed of our thoughts. Also, it is important to train the mind to dwell on present activities in hand, rather than focusing on the past events/ thoughts/ problems. Meditation helps us in bringing rest to mind for sometime, so that it can focus in the present. It also gradually clear the information stored in our subconscious mind which is of no use to us in the present scenario. As we all know, we can only replace the thoughts not remove it. Meditation brings us peace of mind, serenity and transquality.

8. When we befriend God, we give fond memories to friends & family.

Remember- the only person you can change is you. World will automatically change itself with your changed thoughts because others' person behaviour is the reflection of our own mind and when we do efforts to change ourselves, we enjoy the magic of elevated situations as God work on the software of other fellow beings. All are one. The same light is shining in all souls. They are playing their roles as given by God to help us to discover our destiny. So, thanks to all the people, divine lights, coming on & off to our life giving some or other message/ pain or learning. When we meditate on God, He takes away all botherations and fill us with positivity, hope and faith and all tasks get done beautifully automatically.

9. Whenever things does not happen according to our wish, they are happening according to Divine Will

Whenever there is sudden TWIST in our plan, understand it is being rescheduled according to God's will. And only God can give us strength to bear His order. So, my friend, Whenever there is sudden loss of the one we love, Whenever we go through the phase of a prolonged physical illness and mental agony, connect to Supreme God. He listens and give you solutions upfront.

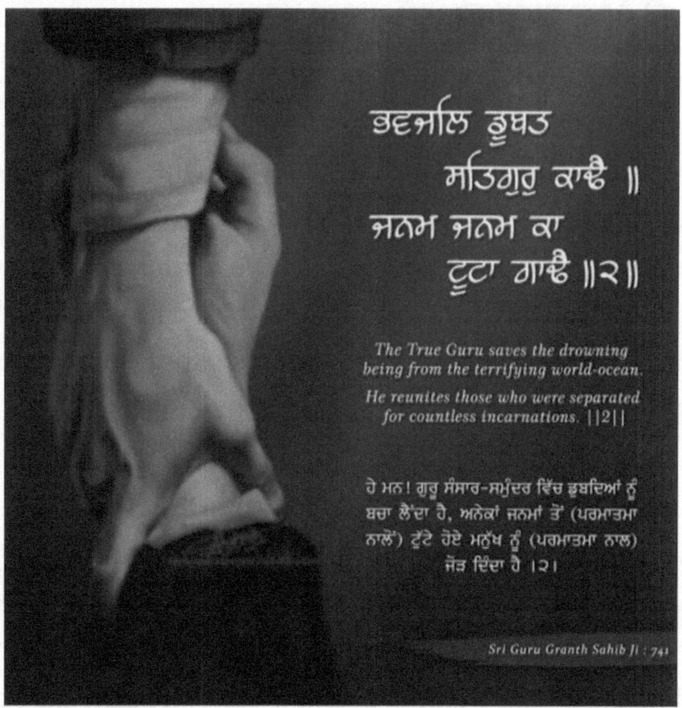

<u>The Conclusion</u>

ਜਾ ਕਉ ਮੁਸਕਲੁ ਅਤਿ ਬਣੈ ਢੋਈ ਕੋਇ ਨ ਦੇਇ ॥
ਜਾ ਕਉ ਮੁਸਕਲੁ ਅਤਿ ਬਣੈ ਢੋਈ ਕੋਇ ਨ ਦੇਇ ॥

Jā kaᵑo muskal at ̱ baṇai dẖoᵑī koᵑe na d ̤eᵑe.

ਲਾਗੁ ਹੋਏ ਦੁਸਮਨਾ ਸਾਕ ਭਿ ਭਜਿ ਖਲੇ ॥

लागू होए दुसमना साक भि भजि खले ॥

Lāgū hoe dusmanā sāk bhė bhaj khale.

ਸਭੋ ਭਜੈ ਆਸਰਾ ਚੁਕੈ ਸਭੁ ਅਸਰਾਉ ॥

सभो भजै आसरा चुकै सभु असराउ ॥

Sabho bhajai āsrā chukai sabh asrāo.

ਚਿਤਿ ਆਵੈ ਓਸੁ ਪਾਰਬ੍ਰਹਮੁ ਲਗੈ ਨ ਤਤੀ ਵਾਉ ॥੧॥

चिति आवै ओसु पारब्रहमु लगै न तती वाउ ॥१॥

Chit āvai os pārbarahm lagai na tatī vāo. ||1||

When you are confronted with terrible hardships, and no one offers you any support, when your friends turn into enemies, and even your relatives have deserted you, and when all support has given way, and all hope has been lost - if you then come to remember the Supreme Lord God, even the hot wind shall not touch you. Our Lord and Master is the Power of the powerless.

He does not come or go; He is Eternal and Permanent. Through the Word of the Guru's Shabad, He is known as True.

If you are weakened by the pains of hunger and poverty, with no money in your pockets, and no one will give you any comfort, and no one will satisfy your hopes and desires, and none of your works is accomplished, if you then come to remember the Supreme Lord God, you shall obtain the eternal kingdom.

When you are plagued by great and excessive anxiety, and diseases of the body; when you are wandering around in all four directions, and you cannot sit or sleep even for a moment - if you come to remember the Supreme Lord God, then your body and mind shall be cooled and soothed.

When you are under the power of sexual desire, anger and worldly attachment, or a greedy miser in love with your wealth; if you have committed the four great sins and other mistakes; even if you are a murderous fiend, who has never taken the time to listen to sacred books, hymns and poetry - if you then come to remember the Supreme Lord God, and contemplate Him, even for a moment, you shall be saved.

LET'S UNDERSTAND, my dear friend;

The moment God (soul) leaves the body it is only a dead plastic body. RIGHT.

God is visible in front of you in from or another. You only need to know we don't associate with the face or body. That is meaningless. Once God (soul) insides us leave the body, body immediately stop all activities. We need to connect to the soul. God is inside each one of us. We need to search it inside by eradicating evil deeds & thoughts. Bodies are masks. God lives inside. So, remember, we are addressing God in everyone not the face mask worn outside. This state of mind can only be achieved by winning five demons.

> *Try to win over the five very powerful demons of*
> *Lust, Anger, Greed, Attachment and Ego;*

We, when live under the influence of any of these egos, our life is pathetic and it leads to miserable destinies like jails, broken homes, hospitals, brothels, trapped by evil persons and distorted relations.

> *Do not do any evil at all; look ahead to the future with foresight.*
> *So throw the dice in such a way, that you shall not lose with your Lord and Master.*
> *Do those deeds which shall bring you profit.*

Now, my friend, it's time to understand these FIVE POWERFUL DEMONS

ATTACHMENT-

Attachment lures you and it is blind. You fail to see any weaknesses |shortcomings of the person you are attached to and hence you keep on getting emotionally trapped. In all relations, there should be detachment in attachment. You are playing your role very fair as a wife, husband, lover, father, mother, daughter, son but at the same time you are not attached to the relation. You love from the core of your heart and are loyal but you are not attached. In this way, other person will grow in your company and your state of mind will also be stable in case that person needs to go away from you temporarily or permanently.

LUST-

It is the most powerful demon and do a great havoc if somebody gets entangled to it. If you get attracted by somebody's looks or touch or soft-sweet words, withdraw yourself from that person immediately otherwise you are most likely to fall into the dangerous trap of lust.And it leads to many heinous crimes too. In committed relation of marriage it is love not lust and being one with each other is a very foundation of this pious institution.

ANGER-

Anger is one word short of danger.It acts in an impulse and destroy many beautiful things -wonderful relations, sweet homes, blissful lives and put us in danger of putting end to many magnificient things of our life.Anger is discussed in detail separately in Chapter 7.

EGO-

It is fragile friend which acts as the biggest barrier in our spiritual,personal and professional growth.The person with high ego is self obsessed and very rigid.He/she is not open to any change in the systems,environment and journey of life.These kind of persons are like stagnant water which stinks and they lose many magical moments of their life because of their high ego. But there is no benefit of gossiping and complaining about such a person rather be more humble over his/her ego to continue your relation with that person.

GREED-

Of course,it lures many a persons when they are bribed or offered lucrative amounts to accomplish any task which should not be done otherwise on ethical grounds.Think fast the moment you are lured by the demon of greed because it is going to rob your honour and grace.Asking good amount of payback of your work is not considered under greed.It is the return gift of your work which you really deserve.

> ***IMPORTANT** is to avoid the company of those who are self willed , are badly trapped in the lure of these demons, hence living life in the direction as envisioned by these powerful demons.Because the consequences of living such a life are dreadful and horrifying.Pray for them to lead a truthful life or render your help to them if possible.*

Holy Sri Guru Granth Sahib Ji,Ang 1417

ਮਨਮੁਖ ਸੇਤੀ ਸੰਗੁ ਕਰੇ ਮੁਹਿ ਕਾਲਖ ਦਾਗੁ ਲਗਾਇ ॥

मनमुख सेती संगु करे मुहि कालख दागु लगाइ ॥

Manmukh setī sang kare muhi kālakh dāg lagāⁿe.

ਮੁਹ ਕਾਲੇ ਤਿਨਹੁ ਲੋਭੀਆਂ ਜਾਸਨਿ ਜਨਮੁ ਗਵਾਇ ॥

मुह काले तिन्ह लोभीआं जासनि जनमु गवाइ ॥

Muh kāle tinh lobhī⁼āʼn jāsan janam gavāⁿe.

Whoever associates with the self-willed people, will have his face blackened and dirtied.

Black are the faces of those greedy people; they lose their lives, and leave in disgrace.

> *Demons of lust, attachment, greed, ego and anger attack us through the behaviour of other human beings in different ways. We need to win over these demons. This is our test and we need to clear it with distinction. These demons will be presented to you on the platter in multiple ways on day to day basis to check your stability and level of elevation in your personality. My friends, believe me, God's name is the shield to protect us from the impact of these demons. It is that strong anti-virus which don't let our thoughts react to the power tricky games of these demons, of course, exhibited through the actions of those around us at home or professional front.*

Holy Sri Guru Granth Sahib Ji, Ang 1192

ਪਾਪ ਕਰੰਤੌ ਨਹ ਸੰਗਾਇ ॥

पाप करंतौ नह संगाइ ॥

Pāp karantou nah sangāᵁe.

ਬਖਿ ਕਾ ਮਾਤਾ ਆਵੈ ਜਾਇ ॥੨॥

बखिु का माता आवै जाइ ॥੨॥

Bikẖ kā māṯā āvai jāᵁe. ||2||

The mortal does not hesitate to commit sins. Intoxicated with poison, he comes and goes in reincarnation.

Acting in egotism and self-conceit, his corruption only increases.

The world is drowning in attachment and greed.

Sexual desire and anger hold the mind in its power.

Even in his dreams, he does not chant the Lord's Name.

Sometimes he is a king, and sometimes he is a beggar.

The world is bound by pleasure and pain.

The mortal makes no arrangements to save himself.

The bondage of sin continues to hold him.

He has no beloved friends or companions.

He himself eats what he himself plants.

God is all Truth, contentment & joy. It is positivity, truth & contentment. It is inside us only that we find the vector of AMRIT, Deep calmness as is found in the depth of ocean.

This is only found when we ASSOCIATE WITH DIVINE BLISS.

Recite God's Name regularly, the first thing in the morning after getting pure and hygienic bath. Sit in the group where God is being remembered fondly.

ਸਤਮੰਗਤਿ ਹਰਿ ਮੇਲਿ ਪਰਭ ਹਰਿ ਨਾਮੁ ਵਸੈ ਮਨਿ ਆਇ ॥
सतसंगति हरि मेलि प्रभ हरि नामु वसै मनि आइ ॥
Satsangat̲ har mel parabẖ har nām vasai man āᵃe.

O Lord, let me join the Sat Sangat, the True Congregation; may the Name of the Lord God abide in my mind.

The filth and pollution of birth and death is washed away, O servant Nanak, singing the Glorious Praises of the Lord.

ABIDE IN THE COMPANY OF HOLY AND SHUN THE COMPANY OF GOSSIPERS AND BACK BITERS.

164

ਚੁਗਲ ਨਿੰਦਕ ਭੁਖੇ ਰੁਲਿ ਮੁਏ ਏਨਾ ਹਥੁ ਨ ਕਿਥਾਉ ਪਾਇ ॥

चुगल निंदक भुखे रुलि मुए एना हथु न किथाऊ पाइ ॥

Chugal nindak bhukhe rul muᵑe enā hath na kithāᵑū pāᵑe.

The gossipers and slanderers shall remain hungry and die, rolling in the dust; their hands cannot reach anywhere.

ਬਾਹਰਿ ਪਾਖੰਡ ਸਭ ਕਰਮ ਕਰਹਿ ਮਨਿ ਹਿਰਦੈ ਕਪਟ ਕਮਾਇ ॥

बाहरि पाखंड सभ करम करहि मनि हिरदै कपटु कमाइ ॥

Bāhar pakhand sabh karam karahi man hirdai kapat kamāᵑe.

Outwardly, they do all the proper deeds, but they are hypocrites; in their minds and hearts, they practice deception and fraud.

ਖੇਤਿ ਸਰੀਰਿ ਜੋ ਬੀਜੀਐ ਸੋ ਅੰਤਿ ਖਲੋਆ ਆਇ ॥

खेति सरीरि जो बीजीऐ सो अंति खलोआ आइ ॥

Khet sarīr jo bījīᵑai so ant khaloᵑā āᵑe.

Whatever is planted in the farm of the body, shall come and stand before them in the end.

> ***And Simply -Your Unique Personal Truthful Goal will be Achieved. We have many true examples of the normal people who befriended God and were henceforth free from the bondages of life and death. God did not consider their background, their past deads , sins and God Almighty , our loving parent, hugged them and elevated them with His love and protection.***

Holy Sri Guru Granth Sahib Ji, Ang 1192

ਸੁਣਿ ਸਾਖੀ ਮਨ ਜਪਿ ਪਿਆਰ ॥
सुणि साखी मन जपि पिआर ॥

Suṇ sākhī man jap pi꠰ār.

Listen to the stories of the devotees, O my mind, and meditate with love.

Ajaamal uttered the Lord's Name once, and was saved.

Baalmeek found the Saadh Sangat, the Company of the Holy.

The Lord definitely met Dhroo.

Ganika the prostitute was saved, when her parrot uttered the Lord's Name.

He delivered the poor Brahmin Sudama out of poverty.

Even the hunter who shot an arrow at Krishna was saved.

Kubija the hunchback was saved, when God placed His Feet on her thumb.

Bidar was saved by his attitude of humility.

The Lord Himself saved the honor of Prahlaad.

Even when she was being disrobed in court, Dropatee's honor was preserved.

Those who have served the Lord, even at the very last instant of their lives, are saved.

O my mind, serve Him, and you shall be carried across to the other side. ||4||

Dhanna served the Lord, with the innocence of a child.

The Guru blessed Baynee with His Divine Illumination.

Jai Dayv gave up his egotism.

Sain the barber was saved through his selfless service.

Do not let your mind waver or wander; do not let it go anywhere.

O my mind, you too shall cross over; seek the Sanctuary of God.

Seeing these ways of Yours, I have dedicated my mind to Your service.

The mortal wanders in reincarnation through countless lifetimes.

Without meditating in remembrance on the Lord, he falls into hell.

Without devotional worship, he is cut apart into pieces.

Without understanding, he is punished by the Messenger of Death.

Meditate and vibrate forever on the Lord of the Universe, O my friend.

Contentment does not come by any endeavors.

All the show of Maya ,worldly pleasures,is just a cloud of smoke.

Feed pure thoughts only
Be confident and Self reliant
Believe in yourself and believe in God's name.

Wishing you a DIVINE BLISS.

My dear friend,
BE YOUR OWN SUNSHINE

Live Free of all grudges, baggages, regrets, judgements and
sorrows.
Live Young forever with a healthy body, clean mind and
shining soul.
Live Happy forever during this journey of life and beyond.

Lead me from death to life, from falsehood to truth
Lead me from despair to hope, from fear to trust
Lead me from hate to love, from war to peace
Let peace fill my heart, my world, my universe

Love n Regards ♡
Your pal,
Gurpreet (Pretty)

Acknowledgements

1. On the foremost, I am filled with affection and gratitude for Loving & Loyal friend of entire humanity, Honourable Holy Sri Guru Granth Sahib ji to provide us with insights to life & beyond through It's divine wisdom which was needed for the content of this book.

2. I'm grateful to respected Sardar Dr. Sant Singh Khalsa for making free availability of his work on internet- 'English translation of Holy Sri Guru Granth Sahib' ji. And likewise to SGPC for their online freely accessible literature on the holiness of marriage.

3. I'm indeed indebted to CA Parvinder Singh, God's gifted child with strong values & intuitive intelligence, my beloved & understanding hubby, for his consistent push to write this book, unconditional love and support for polishing me to what I'm today.

4. I feel blessed to have a brother like S. Satbir Singh Choji, whom I lovingly call as God's favourite child, who not only extended his whole hearted support on every aspect of this book but also have been a holy soul to scrutinize the book with his enlightened magnifying glasses.

5. I fill with joy and gratitude towards God Almighty when I look at my darling children who have been my mentors & motivators throughout my experiencial journey of life. How can I forget their big sacrifices of missing their dear mom in their bubbly childhood while I was away on my Training Sessions. They are

a strong force behind every appreciable achievement of mine. I have proudly named them as Creative Designers of my life.

Our elder dear son, Ruzual Singh, student of IMBA from UNISA, Australia helped me a lot in editing this book with his gifted literary competency and our younger dear son, Kunwar Singh, student of B. Tech. (CSE-AI & ML) from VIT conceptualised various segments of the book with his gifted life skills.

6. I'm all 'Thank You's' to the great writers, motivational trainers and spiritual leaders of the times to provide me with their profound wisdom.

7. I'm thankful to rich & healthy material either freely available on various websites or received in my mail box.

8. I extend my 'warm thank you' to my loving & supportive mother -in -law for being there for our home & family members when I was away for my 'Motivational Talks'.

9. At the same time, I am filled with love for my dear parents who have always entrusted me & motivated me for accomplishing great things in life.

10. I bow and say thank you to all those souls of the Universe who enriched me with wonderful & truthful experiences of life.

11. I'm grateful to all my cherished friends & respected learned souls for sparing their valuable time in reviewing my book & giving their honest remarks.

12. I feel so privileged to be associated with bountiful clients (organisations/persons) for providing me abundant opportunities & therein trusting me to explore and contribute to this world.

13. A big THANKS to all the lucky readers for choosing this book to be their guide in taking them to next level of their life without wasting time on any kind of experimentation.

14. I'm thankful to the dedicated team of NOTION PRESS for beautifully accomplishing the task of publishing this book. A book is a life time toil and a dream come true for any author.

"Thank You Universe"

"Thanku God Almighty for choosing me for this **DIVINE CAUSE** of making positive difference in your dear children's majestic life. "

The Concluding Message

"Live Free Live Young Live Happy"
By S. Satbir Singh

> *The Beginning of Your New Happy and Truthful Baggage Free Young Life*

While reading the book I found it as a very good catalyst which can increase our self confidence, self existence, internal power of mind, uniqueness, internal satisfaction leading to stress free, energetic and happy life. Across whole book one can find many magical quotes which can change one's mind set in a very positive manner.

Author has very well related each topic with teachings of Sahib Sri Guru Granth Sahib Ji by Quoting Gurbani Shabads in each and every topic she has touched. Whole Gurbani is centric on mind and crux of it is the first word Ek Onkar means God is one and we all are part of that one.

MAN TU JOT SAROOP HAI APNA MOOL PEHCHAN. Though we all are unique but we are a part of that one Supreme Power. So just need to recognize it and it's power. All this is very well explained by the author in chapter one 'The Unique You' and in whole book. Next Chapter 'Emotional traps' again author emphasis on state of mind, various traps, ways to get rid of them. Author has used her vast experience of 25 years in the field of training & counseling by the way of quoting different real life case studies and examples in each chapter.

In chapter 3 'It's all in mind'. All about power of mind and wonders it can do…. very well supported by Gurbani… MAN JITE JAG JIT ….. Chapter 4 'Disease and Ease', Author explained in most of the cases root cause of illness is mind. Especially in today's era, over-stress in life is leading to so many diseases. Author has emphasised on holistic healing, healthy and clean stress free environment, self care for well being.

We are living in digital era and carrying whole world in our palms in form of smart phones. But its' all possible because of binary principal of 0 and 1. And its' existence is still on same basic principles discovered years and years ago. Similarly it applies on structure of relationships too. Sex, intimacy and relationships is natural need of human being but we are social and our social upliftment is only because of one institute called marriage, whose base is 1000 of years old and is same across all religions, communities of world. Author has very openly discussed about sex and relationships and problems in society rising due to same and concluded with the importance of a marriage which is base without which humanity can't exist.

In 'Enraged Relationships' author has touched very basic conflicts which come across in our family in day to day life whose consequences are very bad in long term. Ways to handle it and solve it- is very nicely explained. 7 chapter 'Anger Management', "anger for a moment can destroy one's whole life", I found this chapter very useful for ones' who get hyper frequently, technical ways described to deal with anger are very much perfect and useful. And last chapter is the one which should be our mission in life. 'Befriending God'….. Very well supported by lot of Holy Gurbani Shabads. **<u>Every one in this world is selfish except one almighty GOD.</u>**

In last I will mention that this book is about understanding mind, it's problems and issues and getting it united to almighty GOD so that we can live free, live young and live happy.

I recommend this self elevating, psychological and spiritual practical guide to everyone.

With Love & Blessings,
Satbir Singh, PGDBA, BTECH, CAIIB
Branch Head, IDBI Bank Ltd
Spiritual Gurbani Singer (From Amritsar, available on Youtube)

Disclaimer

Dear book owner,

Hope you feel free, young and happy after reading the book. Experiences shared in the book are real, based on the practical aspects of life which I have observed around my surroundings-personal and professional. The names and places of characters are changed to maintain their confidentiality.

The sole purpose of putting my tireless efforts in framing this book is to bring a meaningful visible difference in your life. This is my tribute to the entire humanity of this magnificient universe to gift them a protective shield to live stress free happy life.

Dear readers, I provide my services on basis of the information you (as a person or an organization) provide to me. My role as a Humanitarian is to support and assist you in reaching your own goals but your success depends primarily on your own efforts, motivation, commitment and follow-through. I whole heartedly help you in your paradigm shift towards positive and constructive outcomes but you must agree that I cannot predict and I do not guarantee that you will attain a particular result as you will accept & understand that results differ for each individual. Each individual's results depend on his or her unique background, dedication, desire, motivation, actions and numerous other factors.

I am not, nor am I holding myself to be a Medical Professional ("Medical Provider" or "Mental Health Provider"). I provide information and instructions based on my education, awareness, vast research on human lives and my professional experience of touching more than 2 lac souls in last 25 years.

At last, I wish you a very meaningful, peaceful and bright life. Love, blessings and best wishes,

Dr. Gurpreet Kaur - Motivational Speaker
Ph.D. - Psychology, M.Sc. - Counselling & Psychotherapy, MD - Personnel & Industrial Relations, PGD - Nutrition & Dietetics, B.Sc. - Home Science.

Contact, Speaking or Consulting Inquiries
E-mail: drgkaurb@gmail.com
Linkedin: https://www.linkedin.com/in/dr-gurpreet-kaur-training-consultant-motivational-speaker-7b1bb757/